MAGNETIC NONSENSE

A SHORT HISTORY OF BULLSHIT AT WORK AND HOW TO MAKE IT GO AWAY

PAUL D. SWEENEY

Paul D. Sweeney has asserted his right to be identified as the author of this Work in accordance with the Copyright, Designs and Patents Act 1988

3rd Edition.
First published by Disruption Space Press in 2024

www.disruptionspace.co

A CIP catalogue record for this book is available from the British Library

ISBN 978-1-0685310-4-0

For Nicole

PREFACE

The driving force behind this book is the idea that liberating people and organisations from the sea of mindless nonsense we are drowning in at work could be game-changing. The journey we will take uncovers the origins of nonsense at work and explains why it's so universal. Along the way, evidence will lead us to some surprising conclusions, including:

- Our susceptibility to nonsense, driven by our *aversion to uncertainty*, our *drive for sense-making*, and our tendency for *belief perseverance*, has an evolutionary basis.
- Our belief systems about work have been warped by an industry of pseudoscience research, popular 'success' literature, consultant-generated management fads and the shallow soundbites of fake gurus.
- We've long been conditioned to blame culture as the convenient culprit for all corporate bad behaviour. But there's far more compelling evidence that power and hierarchy should be our prime suspects.

Hierarchy is also implicated in the creation of bullshit jobs, which by some estimates make up over 40% of white collar roles.

- Visions are not visionary. Purpose is meaningless unless it can be delivered profitably, and corporate values are beyond pointless.
- Wellbeing initiatives don't increase wellbeing. Performance appraisals cannot be trusted. Diversity initiatives can increase bias and miss the bigger picture, and employee engagement surveys are flawed and infantilising.
- Thanks to management education (MBA teaching in particular), a rational and narrow lens on efficiency has killed many possibilities for joy and magic at work.
- Governance, as provided by boards of directors and auditors, is a complete illusion and an outrageous waste of money.
- Meetings are not only an annoying waste of time and energy, but they also lead to fake consensus for very dumb ideas.
- Almost all transformation efforts are designed from a starting point of outdated and overly rational perspectives that make success highly unlikely.
- Artificial intelligence will soon make everything immeasurably worse if we're not extremely careful.

The more nonsense we can eliminate, the more time and energy we will have to do something genuinely exciting and innovative. Employees, shareholders, and society as a whole stand to gain.

There is hope that we can make genuine progress by adopting an ethos of humanity over efficiency, reinventing HR to be useful, developing our critical thinking and design skills, and dealing with the downsides of power and hierarchy. As we will see, there is enough evidence to point us in the right direction.

If we get this right, the only losers will be the comedy writers who, for decades, have relied on the comic absurdity of work for their material. A shame, but a price worth paying, in my view.

THE NONSENSE FRAMEWORK

As we will discover, there's an easy way to create multi-billion dollar industries of nonsense by exploiting cognitive patterns hard-wired early in human evolution. These patterns include our *aversion to uncertainty*, our *drive for sense-making*, and our tendency for *belief perseverance*.

Step 1. Trigger our aversion to uncertainty

"Do you know the secrets of success in business and life? How are you going to succeed without them?"

Step 2. Create the illusion of sense-making

"This research into famous billionaires' habits, routines and thinking patterns explains why they succeeded. These are the universal laws of success."

Step 3. Promise control over the future

"Buy this book, obey these secret universal laws, and you too will achieve incredible success in work and life."

Once we're hooked, our evolutionary preference for *belief perseverance* means we make little effort to apply critical thinking or seek disconfirming evidence, even when, 12 months later, we inevitably don't seem to be much closer to becoming a famous billionaire...

Stupid people do stupid things, but people who are smart enough can do something really stupid.

— ROBERT CHARLES WILSON

CONTENTS

PART VI
A GOOD PLACE TO END? AN OPEN LETTER TO THE CEO

INTRODUCTION

The past 100 years have seen extraordinary progress in almost every field of human endeavour. Humans have decoded DNA, split atoms, soared into the skies, voyaged to the moon and dived to the bottom of our deepest oceans. With teams racing to create new satellite networks in sub-space, soon there will be nowhere left on the planet where you won't be able to waste your days letting social media algorithms form your opinions and manipulate you into buying more stuff you don't need.

But one hugely important dimension of our lives has mysteriously failed to evolve. Work has somehow defeated the promise of progress and has resolutely remained part tragedy, part comedy. This failure to evolve might have been understandable had organisations reached a peak of evolution, like the crocodile, so perfectly designed for its habitat that it has little pressure to evolve further. But that is not the case.

Our days at work are filled with endless meetings and activities. We have little time to reflect on the very nature of work. But if we could freeze time, step off the treadmill and become a detached observer for long enough, we would see that much of our activity is pointless, and some is downright absurd. Most of us have a slightly uneasy sense that life at work often seems to involve pretending that all kinds of nonsense are somehow perfectly sane. This nonsense seems to have magnetic qualities, a forcefield that holds us all in a strange dimension where independence of thought is rare, and 'best practice' reliably leads to worst outcomes.

Dysfunction is everywhere. Employee engagement is dismal across the globe. Corporate greed and scandals are our daily bread. Many of us are in a constant state of stress at work, and some have burnt out. There's an epidemic of work-related mental health issues. The bad news is that your organisation is massively dysfunctional. The good news is that it's not unique.

Many billions have been wasted on endless interventions—transformation, restructuring, management consultants, leadership gurus, new technologies, and astronomical remuneration for superstar CEOs. Why have all these efforts failed to move the dial? Why do almost all organisations seem destined to be mediocre at best?

From blind acceptance of hierarchy to pseudoscience research, management fads, and the soundbites of self-proclaimed gurus, we are continuously sold simplistic solutions that promise to improve everything. But they never do. They simply trap us in a doom loop of nonsense that conspires to protect our organisations from any assault by common sense.

To understand how we got here will require us to weave together strands from diverse disciplines - systems thinking, complexity theory, anthropology, psychology, social science and behavioural economics. It turns out that there are multiple factors at play, internal and external forces that converge on the world of work and create self-reinforcing loops and belief systems that ensure we make the same mistakes repeatedly. This is the story of how we got to here, why we keep falling for the same nonsense, and what we can do to change the misguided belief systems that collectively prevent us from reaching a better work future.

PART I

HOW DID WE END UP IN THIS MESS?

Our comforting conviction that the world makes sense rests on a secure foundation: our almost unlimited ability to ignore our ignorance.

— DANIEL KAHNEMAN

1

NONSENSE & THE HUMAN CONDITION: EVOLUTIONARY HANGOVERS

We live in a world primarily shaped by the technologies we invented, where our domination as a species is now absolute. But in one curious respect, we remain constrained by our biology. Our human brains have been unable to evolve at the same dramatic pace at which we have transformed our environment. Humankind has broken evolution.

Our brains continue to operate in ways that were hard-wired many thousands of years ago. We still have an automatic physiological response to acute stress (often called the 'fight or flight' response). Without consciously thinking about it, our bodies automatically react by, among other things, diverting blood flow to the muscles in anticipation of action, increasing heart rate and blood pressure, pumping fuel into the bloodstream from the liver (in the form of glucose and fats), and increasing respiration to help burn the extra fuel. Our pupils even dilate to give us better vision.

But there are three other areas where evolution has left its mark on our cognition – the fundamental way our brain processes information about the world around us. The first is a marked *aversion to uncertainty*; the second is an innate *drive for sense-making*; and the third is *belief perseverance* – persistently maintaining beliefs in the face of new information that strongly contradicts them. And it is the combination of these three evolutionary hangovers that leaves us so susceptible to nonsense today.

For almost 90% of our human history, we lived as hunter-gatherers with an existence far less complex than life in the 21st century. Back then, life was sporadically dangerous but otherwise broadly predictable. Our brains evolved to be superb at recognising patterns and storing the responses in our subconscious, so they became habitual and automatic behaviours. This freed up our conscious minds to pay attention to anything out of the ordinary, which was more than likely to signal danger. Have you ever arrived home after your commute without remembering anything about your drive? If so, this is because you were effectively on autopilot with your subconscious brain doing the heavy lifting.

Given our brain's predisposition towards pattern-making and habit-forming, we evolved to perceive uncertainty as a threat. Uncertainty equals danger. Your brain can no longer keep you safe if it can't anticipate what's coming next. Not only can this trigger the 'fight or flight' response, but researchers have established that it can also affect our ability to focus and cooperate and even reduce our sense of well-being[1].

In a fascinating study[2] at the University College London Institute of Neurology, researchers recruited volunteers to play a digital game in which rocks appeared on the screen, and they had to guess whether a snake was hiding under them. If a snake was revealed upon turning over the rock, they received a mild but unpleasant electric shock. As they played more, they learned which rocks were most likely to have a snake hidden underneath them, but those odds changed as the game progressed, generating fluctuating levels of uncertainty. Using a highly sophisticated computational learning model, the researchers were able to estimate the level of uncertainty each participant experienced at various points in the game. This was then plotted against the participants' stress levels at those points, tracked by a combination of changes to salivary cortisol, pupil diameter, and perspiration. The results were surprising:

"Using our model, we could predict how stressed our subjects would be not just from whether they got shocks but how much uncertainty they had about them," says lead author Archy de Berker. "Our experiment allows us to draw conclusions about the effect of uncertainty on stress. It turns out that it's much worse not knowing if you will get a shock than knowing you definitely will or won't."[*]

Exposure to persistent perceived uncertainty (even if the perception of uncertainty was unfounded) turns out to be incredibly dangerous to our health. A study across two large, nationally representative samples of U.S. adults[3] found that persistent perceived job insecurity was an even stronger predictor of poor health outcomes than either smoking or high blood pressure (two of the three primary factors in coronary heart disease, the leading cause of death in the US). Other research into the effects of uncertainty points to an intolerance of uncertainty (the tendency to react negatively to uncertain situations) as a factor in the rise of General Anxiety Disorder among adolescents[4]. Uncertainty, if left unresolved for long enough, could be so debilitating it might even be fatal. No wonder we dislike it so much.

---

[*] This may explain why those 'creeping' train delays, where the information keeps changing, seem far more stressful than the certainty that your train is cancelled. It may also explain why being dumped by someone you started dating and liked seemed a blessed relief after days of wondering whether it was going anywhere.

Our drive for sense-making also characterises the human condition. Writing in the *Journal of Economic Behavior & Organization*[5], Nick Chater (Professor of Behavioural Science at Warwick Business School) and George Loewenstein (Professor of Economics and Psychology at Carnegie Mellon University) argue that the human drive for sense-making is hugely under-appreciated and should be considered as: "analogous to better-known drives such as hunger, thirst and sex."

Their review of the evidence of this sense-making drive across a diverse range of psychology research leads them to conclude that sense-making is a fundamental human motivation that drives us to seek simplified representations of the world. Once we accept these simplified representations as the truth, we are reluctant to be challenged on them as that would pull us back to the state of uncertainty we find so uncomfortable.

The sense-making drive goes back to the dawn of human history, as we searched for explanations to make sense of our existence, how we came to be, and how the universe was created. Creation myths - stories that explain how the earth and its creatures were formed along with the sun and the moon - are widespread across early human cultures, suggesting that the drive for sense-making is universal and hard-wired into our brains from the early stages of human development. Maybe our ancestors knew more than we thought because many of these myths describe how the world originated from a void or chaos into order[6] – remarkably consistent with the 'Big Bang' theory[7] of the origin of the universe developed by physicists many thousands of years later.

This drive for sense-making is evident in almost every area of our lives. We constantly take a 'reductionist' approach, seeking to simplify complex situations and interactions. Unfortunately, this means we tend to accept oversimplified explanations at face value, leaving us open to being easily manipulated by those who stand to gain from our hard-wired naivety.

One aspect of our lives that we are increasingly concerned about is the trajectory of our health. Non-communicable diseases (NCDs) such as cardiac disease, cancer, chronic respiratory diseases and diabetes are now the leading cause of death globally, killing over 41 million people each year, according to the World Health Organisation[8]. One of the primary factors in this global rise of NCDs is a diet high in ultra-processed foods[9] with high sodium and low nutrient levels. Given the complexity of these diseases, we face a high level of uncertainty about how to protect our future health. This uncertainty, kept high by endless media coverage and advertising, provides a bountiful opportunity for nutritional supplement manufacturers, whose global sales were valued at around USD 337 billion in 2022 and are forecast to reach over USD 647 billion by 2030[10]. A 2023 survey of US adults found that 59% of adults over 20 took supplements regularly, rising to 70% over 60.

We know that consuming some foods (primarily fruits, vegetables, nuts and legumes) can help protect us against these NCDs[11]. However, the mechanisms by which they do so are highly complex and still not fully understood. These foods contain many compounds, including vitamins, minerals, fatty acids, amino acids, and polyphenols. Over 8,000 different types of polyphenols alone have been discovered. Research (often funded by supplement manufacturers) has aimed to simplify this complexity by isolating so-called 'active compounds' in these foods to put them in a pill and sell them back to us.

Because of our growing uncertainty about health, supplement manufacturers with substantial advertising budgets have been able to convince us that these pills provide a kind of insurance policy against the effects of our poor lifestyle choices. For most people, taking multivitamins or other supplements in the belief that we are protecting our health is a far easier option than making wholesale diet and lifestyle changes.

In his groundbreaking book *How Not to Die*[12], Dr Michael Greger points out that most consumers of these supplements seem unaware that they are typically not regulated like medicines. In most countries, the only regulations they are subject to cover the preparation and packaging of food. Unlike approved drugs, there is no requirement to demonstrate any beneficial health effect or to show that they can safely interact with other medications. Marketing claims for these supplements range from disingenuous to outrageous. Here's an example from one popular website in the UK selling dietary supplements:

"Organic moringa powder is also great for your liver – it helps protect the organ from damage and can even reverse the damage already done.*"

Supplement manufacturers don't even have to prove that the ingredients match the label on the bottle. In 2015, the New York State Attorney General's office accused four of the country's biggest retailers (Walmart, GNC, Target & Walgreens) of selling fraudulent herbal supplements[13] – stating that four out of every five products they had tested from these retailers contained none of the herbs listed on their ingredients label. Instead, they had cheap bulk fillers and, in some cases, even household plants. It gets worse. Even if the bottle contained the ingredients listed on the label, there's usually no evidence that supplements deliver health benefits. Many can even be harmful in high doses, like vitamin C, which can cause painful kidney stones if you ingest too much too often[14]. Multiple long-term studies of multivitamin and multimineral supplements have shown no overall

---

* Not quite the whole picture. Studies have shown that overconsumption of moringa can actually cause liver failure.

benefit to mortality, leading to calls from scientists[15] to: "Stop wasting money on vitamin and mineral supplements."

So, why do most of these supplements appear to have little to no effect, while the whole foods they were isolated from are proven to be beneficial for our health? It turns out that the 'reductionist' approach to try and simplify a very complex set of interactions doesn't work. Despite many advances in research, the critical learning for scientists in this field is that we are nowhere close to fully understanding the mechanisms by which some compounds affect our bodies.

As Greger points out, when you eat broccoli, for example, you are not only getting sulforaphane (the 'active compound' in broccoli supplements) but fibre, vitamins (A, C and K), minerals (calcium, potassium, iron), and other bioactive compounds such as glucosinolates, quercetin, and indole-3-carbinol, all of which have been shown to have significant health-promoting effects[16]. All of these interact with each other and with other molecules and compounds from other foods. Scientists have also recently discovered that foods contain something called microRNAs, compounds that can even regulate the expression of our genes, in some cases protecting us from DNA damage. Victor Ambros and Gary Ruvkun were jointly awarded a Nobel Prize in 2024 for this discovery[17].

Trying to isolate individual active compounds in such a vastly complex landscape is a fool's errand. But our drive to try and simplify the world means we keep trying the same thing repeatedly, even when evidence shows that this is not a helpful approach. Advice from leading experts is to get your nutrients from a diet rich in whole food plant-based sources. But once we are hooked on the story that supplements are our insurance policy for bad lifestyle choices, it's hard to get us to critically examine that story – despite the readily accessible body of evidence.

As we will see, the approach taken in decades of organisational and leadership research has the same fundamental flaw. We have tried to isolate individual 'factors' to concoct prescriptions for success, and it simply hasn't worked. And just like the dietary supplement industry, 'leadership gurus' can market the 'secrets of business success' with no requirement to prove that there is any evidence whatsoever to support their claims.

This is where we meet the third factor of interest in the human condition: *Belief perseverance*. Our tendency to hold on to our beliefs in the face of insurmountable evidence to the contrary was famously illustrated in the book published in 1956 by social psychologists Leon Festinger, Henry Riecken, and Stanley Schachter: *When Prophecy Fails - A Social and Psychological Study of a Modern Group That Predicted the Destruction of the World*[18,*].

Festinger infiltrated a cult called the Seekers, which believed that aliens from the planet Clarion would arrive in flying saucers to save them from an impending apocalypse. Their leader, Dorothy Martin, claimed to be receiving telepathic messages from the aliens, who she called the Guardians. According to Martin, the Guardians had warned her that this apocalypse would occur before dawn on December 21st, 1954. In preparation for their space travel, some cult members ended relationships, quit their jobs and gave away all their worldly possessions.

As the sun rose on December 21st, the apocalypse failed to materialise. Festinger observed something fascinating. When faced with what he termed the 'cognitive dissonance' caused by the prophecy's failure, the most fervent believers in the group became even more committed to their beliefs. They began to court more publicity and developed various explanations for the

---

* Still one of the coolest book titles ever.

prophecy's failure. Subsequently, they became convinced that the Guardian's UFOs would appear on Christmas Eve 1954 and persevered in their beliefs despite the inevitable second disappointment.

The Seekers dispersed shortly afterwards, but after a brief spell in Peru, Martin founded a new group in Arizona, The Association of Sananda and Sanat Kumara. Offshoots of these groups are still active today. One, the Solar Star Command[19], has a "Healing Mission to free Humanity from the Matrix* by 2045." So, at least the next major cognitive dissonance event has been pushed out by a couple of decades.

In our discussion on sense-making, we touched on creation myths as the earliest efforts to make sense of the universe and our place in it. Many Christians still believe that the creation myth is a factual account of how the world came to be – that the world was created in just seven days, less than 10,000 years ago. A 2019 survey of US adults found that only 34% of Republican voters believed in evolution[20], compared to 83% of Democratic voters. About 54% of the survey respondents supported the idea of evolution in 2019.

This is markedly different to the UK, where over 70% of people support the science backing the theory of evolution[21]. People from the UK are often surprised by the extent to which creationist theories are popular globally. For example, *The Journal of Creation*[22] is a publication that aims to prove that the earth is only 6,000 years old. Many diverse areas are explored, with article titles such as "Unusual accumulation of dinosaurs in Italy better explained by Noah's Flood". The organisation behind the journal, Creation Ministries International (CMI), claims subscribers in 170 countries. CMI and another creationist

---

* Apparently a computer-generated reality in which we are all trapped. I wonder where they got that idea.

organisation called (somewhat ironically perhaps) Truth in Science attracted the displeasure of the UK's scientific establishment in 2011, with over 30 prominent scientists (including Sir David Attenborough and Richard Dawkins) signing a letter to the government claiming that the two creationist organisations were: "touring the UK and presenting themselves as scientists and their creationist views as science." The letter went on to say: "Creationism and intelligent design are not scientific theories, but they are portrayed as scientific theories by some religious fundamentalists...there should be enforceable statutory guidance that they may not be presented as scientific theories in any publicly funded school."

Perhaps the most interesting aspect of these debates is that those who maintain firmly held creationist beliefs appear entirely unmoved by the ever-increasing body of scientific research and evidence to the contrary. It simply makes no difference. No amount of new information will change their minds. Our drive for sense-making and our dislike of uncertainty confine us to this illogical state of belief perseverance, where new and possibly even vital information is ignored.

Because of the interplay between our dislike of uncertainty and our attraction to simplicity, our explanations of the past tend to gloss over the 'uncertain' random variables. Factors such as luck, accident, a chance meeting, and even change in the weather (the deciding factor in some of history's most famous military victories[23]). We refuse to acknowledge that the world is complex, messy and unpredictable.

Other prominent thinkers concur. The Nobel Prize-winning economist Daniel Kahneman came to a similar conclusion in his bestselling book *Thinking Fast & Slow*[24], pointing out that the illusion of understanding the past leads to the further illusion that we can predict and control the future. Kahneman noted that this was comforting because it avoided the uncertainty generated by admitting the world was messy and complex. He observed that many popular business books were based on feeding this comforting illusion.

Rory Sutherland is a huge personality in the UK's advertising industry and a powerful orator who never fails to inspire and entertain. Vice Chairman of the Ovilgy & Mather group and an early pioneer of digital advertising, Rory is well known for championing behavioural economics and is the author of *Alchemy: The Power of Ideas That Don't Make Sense*[25]. Rory has spoken extensively about the need to embrace 'messy' and stop pretending that the world is neater than it is. In his opening addresses at the 2023 Nudgestock (billed as the world's largest festival of behavioural science and creativity), Rory pointed out:

"90% of success in business is actually highly messy, non-linear, non-directional, but most of the effort in business is devoted to pretending that's not true."

And in that pretence, we continually fail to learn from the past. The most fascinating thing is that the pretence continues unquestioned and expands over time, even when credible evidence emerges that it is nonsensical. So, with our 'lizard' brains craving relief from uncertainty through overly simplistic explanations of the past and overconfident illusions of control over the future - the conditions are set perfectly for nonsense to thrive. And it certainly has.

* * *

Back to the world of work. Almost all large companies carry on with a bewildering array of activities that make no demonstrable difference, apart from wasting time and money and generally annoying their employees. Let's take one example. Wellbeing. Hyped by consultants who influenced government policy and executive teams worldwide, 'wellbeing' became a hot trend (otherwise known as a management fad) around 2017. Deloitte and the UK's Chartered Institute for Personnel Development (CIPD) launched rival workplace wellbeing surveys shortly afterwards. Executives got very uncomfortable when many employees reported that they weren't feeling 'very well' in these surveys. Large organisations appointed Chief Wellbeing Officers, recruited wellbeing teams and hired costly wellbeing consultants who suddenly appeared on the scene from nowhere. A veritable avalanche of activity ensued, with some organisations creating over eighty different wellbeing interventions - everything from 'duvet days' to workplace yoga, guided meditation apps, one-on-one mindfulness coaching, sound wave healing, cupping, and dog petting.

Millions of employees received mildly patronising missives about taking action to improve their mental health, no doubt causing a rise in anxiety amongst those who were previously fine. Annual reports and senior leadership conferences were full of 'wellbeing strategy' presentations highlighting what a great and caring employer the organisation had suddenly become.

There was only one slightly inconvenient problem with all of this. It turns out that there's no evidence that any of these interventions increase employee wellbeing. Multiple research studies have come to the same conclusions. Oxford University's Wellbeing Centre published research in 2023 on the effect of mental health interventions across 143 UK companies with 27,932 employees[26]. The report's author, Dr William Fleming, says:

"The analysis estimates the effect of a range of common initiatives, including mindfulness, resilience training, stress management and wellbeing apps. No evidence is found to demonstrate that these strategies improve worker mental health across multiple employee mental health measures. This suggests that recent critical literature is right to be concerned and that convenient wellbeing strategies should be given less financial and institutional support."

The report also found evidence that one category of wellness intervention, stress and resilience training, actually increases stress levels and leads to a corresponding decrease in wellbeing. Dr Fleming goes on to bemoan the poor quality of research in the field, going so far as to specifically call out Deloitte's research and their declaration of an overwhelmingly positive business case for investment in wellbeing, saying that "their ad hoc selection process and inability to identify valid studies undermines return-on-investment estimates that are widely and uncritically shared in public media and academic literature."

Let me paraphrase the above in non-academic language: It's complete bullshit.

The message from Deloitte (and others) was beautifully crafted to exploit our dislike of uncertainty and drive for sense-making. It's little wonder that it quickly became a top executive focus globally. Let's deconstruct it.

Step one: *Trigger our aversion to uncertainty*. Our research shows that many employees should be considered at risk of high stress, burnout, underperformance, and leaving. The future of your organisation is uncertain.

Step 2. *Create the illusion of sense-making*: It's all the organisation's fault (i.e., your fault as leaders). You've allowed this to happen through your uncaring approach as an employer with long hours, demanding managers, pressured tasks, etc. What were you thinking?*

Step 3. *Promise control over the future*: We can help you to fix your wellbeing through this range of interventions. Here's the

---

* Note that the explanation completely ignored the complexity of individual personal lives, circumstances and predispositions to mental health issues and discounts any responsibility for the individual to look after their own wellbeing.

cast-iron business case for the investment. Trust us; we know what we are doing. This will cost you £X but will return almost £5X.

Despite having their research methodology so publicly slammed, as recently as May 2024, Deloitte still claimed that: "For every £1 spent on supporting the mental health and well-being of their workforce, employers get (on average) about £4.70 back in increased productivity."[27] Shameless.

Having so publicly committed to wellbeing and wasted vast amounts of time and cash, most organisations have ignored the growing evidence that their approaches are ineffective. The wellbeing train rolls on, seemingly unstoppable. The only good news in the middle of all this nonsense is that one type of intervention has more promise. Multiple studies have shown that training managers to be more supportive of their employees' autonomy led to their employees reporting greater job satisfaction, higher levels of wellbeing and, interestingly, more positive and trusting attitudes toward top management[28]. A better use of time and money, perhaps? More on the case for increased autonomy later.

Just to be clear, I fully support the idea that we should collectively seek ways to support better health and happiness at work. However, the ways in which we do so must be evidence-based. Unfortunately, organisations and their leadership teams appear to be incredibly resistant to evidence-based practice. Our dislike of uncertainty seems to defeat common sense every time. We've created a system where the rewards for overconfidence and blind conformity hugely outweigh the rewards for intelligent questioning and challenge. As we will see next, this has happened since the birth of the modern organisation.

2

CONTROL & COERCION: ORIGINS OF THE MODERN ORGANISATION

In his excellent book *Sapiens: A Brief History of Humankind*[1], Yuval Noah Harari makes a compelling argument that humans evolved into the planet's dominant species because of the unique development of language, followed by what he refers to as a 'cognitive revolution' (c.70,000 years ago) that allowed humans to form shared myths, beliefs, and stories, which in turn enabled us to collaborate flexibly in large groups.

Before modern organisations existed, our models for group work were essentially military or religious, or in some cases both, like the ill-fated Knights of Templar*. In a stroke of genius, this entrepreneurial religious-military order used 'faith' both to leverage donations to fund their crusades and to gain tax exemptions on vast land holdings and plundered treasure. Like today's super-rich, the more wealth they accumulated, the less tax they paid.

---

* The Knights Templar (formal name *The Poor Fellow-Soldiers of Christ and of the Temple of Solomon*) was a French military order of the Catholic faith, and one of the wealthiest organisations in Western Christianity. They were founded c. 1119 to defend pilgrims on their way to Jerusalem, with their headquarters located on the Temple Mount, and existed for nearly two hundred years.

Unfortunately, their business model was so successful they became a target for the jealous King Philip IV of France, who persuaded Pope Clement V to have them arrested on trumped-up charges of heresy, idolatry, and homosexuality. Today, a walker along the Seine in Paris can find a plaque under the Pont Neuf marking where the last Knights were executed in 1314. Being the CEO was a little riskier then. These days, the punishment for corporate greed or bad behaviour is a multi-million-pound payoff, an opportunity to improve your gardening skills, and a tasty portfolio of non-executive roles shortly afterwards.

A shared starting point for these models was a belief that people were inherently untrustworthy and needed to be controlled and coerced to do work. They, therefore, relied heavily on rigid hierarchy, top-down command, and severe disincentives for non-compliance. These disincentives included incarceration, excommunication, execution, and, my personal favourite, everlasting torment in hell. The Catholic version of hierarchy even included 'Papal Infallibility', a brilliant construct for the Pope (effectively the CEO), who was deemed divinely unable to be wrong and whose decisions could never be questioned. Nice work.

Before the First Industrial Revolution in the late 18th and early 19th centuries, most work was artisanal, often carried out in the home, either alone or with relatively small numbers of other artisans. The landscape changed during the First Industrial Revolution as factories were developed and workers migrated from the land. Later in the 20th century, a massive wave of innovation resulted from the Second World War, leading to explosive post-war growth across industries, many brand new. Aviation, television, computing, and automotive are but some examples. Many of the organisations founded in this era were led by former military personnel, who replicated the hierarchical models of their military experience in designing organisation structures and leadership constructs.

And with few exceptions, we haven't come very far since. In more recent decades, there's been a stunning lack of innovation in how organisations are run. Most large organisations have converged on identical approaches to pretty much everything. They have the same hierarchical structure, concentrating massive decision-making power in a small group of leaders. They have the same governance structures. The same board committees. They share similar corporate values. Executive compensation schemes are cut-and-paste. HR policies are indistinguishable. Annual reports look like they were all written using the same template. Their CEOs give carefully manicured speeches about the same things, desperately trying not to offend any minority group, no matter how small or obscure, in case they are 'cancelled'. Large corporates have essentially become a bland amorphous mass. And because of this homogeneity, they all appear to be dysfunctional in very similar ways.

In my career, I've worked in and advised companies in many sectors, from aviation to utilities to banking and real estate. I've seen how organisations work in the UK, Europe, the US and the Middle East. Societal differences aside, the same poor thinking is ubiquitous. Like the boy in *The Sixth Sense*[2] movie who began to see dead people everywhere, I began to see the same nonsense everywhere.

All the large organisations I encountered were strangely familiar. They used the same annoying buzzwords and jargon. They followed the same accepted wisdom, even though it clearly wasn't working. They hired the same consultants and experts to tell them to do the same things. Original thinking, which may have been a feature early in their evolution, was now largely extinct.

Customers were regularly astounded by how difficult these

organisations were to deal with. They encountered frustrating processes, errors, delays, and an all-too-familiar sense of disappointment. Simple requests became incredibly difficult, involving queuing for hours on helplines to speak with agents thousands of miles away who had no idea how to solve the issue. A few savvy customers found it far more efficient to email the CEO directly and that the organisation could instantly resolve these complaints through some dark magic.

Frontline employees felt unsupported, undervalued and underpaid. Middle managers were stressed and ineffective, often burning out. Leaders seemed oddly detached from reality, spending their time discussing abstract concepts like 'values' and 'culture' - which seemed to get more attention than solving problems that employees or customers cared about in the real world.

Senior management conferences featured rallying keynotes from famous ex-athletes or retired football managers, as if sharing their experiences from contexts that had little in common with the work lives of their audience would somehow catalyse a change for the better in the collective brain. This made no difference whatsoever other than as a welcome temporary respite from the drudgery of their daily work life. Any bump in enthusiasm vanished within a day or two as things snapped back to normal dysfunction like a released elastic band.

As soon as one restructure finished badly, another was launched before people could catch their breath or clear up the mess from the previous one. Performance initiatives and incentive schemes came and went with dizzying frequency, dreamt up by senior managers who seemed to have no idea how the organisation worked. Employees quickly worked out how to game the incentives, focusing more on maximising their rewards than delivering the value the incentives supposedly drove them towards.

New corporate values were periodically launched with tremendous fanfare. Many trinkets adorned with the new values were distributed to the masses in the apparent belief that this would somehow change the employees' behaviours to match better the rose-tinted descriptions of 'living our values' made up by someone in the HR team.

But fundamentally, very little changed despite the frenzied effort and costly activity. Five years after being involved in a project at a major UK bank, I returned to speak with some of the project team. In those five years, there had been another half a dozen restructures and countless change initiatives. When asked how things were now, the answer was: "Pretty much the same, just a bit worse than before."

One of the team had replicated the list that psychologist and author Ben Dattner described[3] seeing on a co-worker's cubicle wall at Republic National Bank of New York:

The six phases of a project:

1. Enthusiasm
2. Disillusionment
3. Panic
4. Search for the guilty
5. Punishment of the innocent
6. Rewards for the uninvolved

Every time there was a fallout from another change project that failed to deliver on the lofty aspirations laid out in the launch PowerPoint presentation, this list was a source of great hilarity. Strangely, nobody in the senior leadership ranks questioned why the accepted wisdom didn't work. Nobody suggested departing from standard ways of thinking and operating to test anything new. The rewards for conformity and pretending everything was under control vastly outweighed the rewards for attempting to challenge the status quo.

But here's the interesting thing: These organisations were

run by competent, highly paid, highly incentivised leadership teams. They didn't want their employees or customers to have a poor experience, so they spent millions of pounds on the latest leadership development trends. They jumped on the newest fads, everything from 'Lean Six Sigma' to 'leading with purpose'. But in every case I encountered, all these things somehow failed to move the dial. It was all just nonsense.

* * *

And this endemic nonsense provides excellent inspiration for comedy writers. The huge TV hit *The Office,* created in 2001 by Ricky Gervais and Stephen Merchant, starred Gervais as David Brent, a delusional, self-promoting middle manager. The show went on to have wildly successful international versions in countries as diverse as India, Japan, and Saudi Arabia, with the US version alone winning 51 awards and 197 nominations[4]. Regardless of the country, each version had an almost identical script, storyline and set of characters. It seems that the tragicomic nature of life at work has become universal.

This may also explain the enduring appeal of Scott Adam's *Dilbert* cartoon strip[5] , which poked fun at the absurdity of modern organisational life. Although the strip was dropped in 2023 because of personal remarks made by Adams, at its height, it was published daily in over 2,000 newspapers in 65 countries and 25 languages. Seemingly oblivious to the irony, The European Foundation for Management Development ranked Adams 21st on its 2007 list of the 50 most influential management thinkers worldwide.

But while it is easy to laugh at the nonsense that pervades our working lives, it seems strangely hard to kill any of it. It has magnetic qualities. As we will discover next, powerful and self-interested forces of conformity maintain the status quo, making our organisations virtually impregnable to better thinking.

If you only read the books that everyone else is reading, you can only think what everyone else is thinking.

— HARUKI MURAKAMI

3

POPULAR DECEPTIONS:
PSEUDOSCIENCE & SUCCESS BOOKS

To fully understand the origins of the nonsense afflicting the modern workplace, we must journey back to the 1950s and 1960s when new disciplines such as organisational behaviour and management research emerged. These disciplines sought to understand the inner workings of organisations and determine how to make them more efficient. This early research gave rise to the 'management guru' phenomenon, epitomised by Charles Handy and W. Edwards Deming, who developed hugely influential leadership and management theories.

These theories had the same philosophical foundation as the religious and military models that preceded them, namely:

1. Leaders can predict and control the future of the organisation.
2. Organisations behave as rational, predictable systems.
3. The right leaders with the right structures, processes, and incentives will inevitably produce the optimal outputs.

This philosophy fits our nonsense framework perfectly, reducing uncertainty, providing the illusion of sense-making, and promising control over future outcomes. Despite much criticism, this philosophy still forms the foundation of almost all approaches to organisational research and leadership training today.

If you believed that leaders could determine and control the future, then you would focus your research efforts on trying to identify and isolate the leadership 'behaviours' or 'characteristics' that were predictive of success (not dissimilar to the 'active compound' approach in useless nutritional supplements). You would seek to do the same with organisational structures, processes, incentives, performance management, etc.

And, of course, this is precisely what has happened. But these are hugely biased starting points. Leaders can have an impact, not because they are superior beings, but because of their pure concentration of decision-making power. We have unwittingly created a vast pseudoscience industry by assuming that leadership is the dominant variable and that we can simplify the complexity of organisational life and solve all organisational problems by just getting the 'right' leaders in place with a repeatable framework. There's simply no evidence to support this belief.

In other areas of academic and scientific research, this kind of bias was largely killed off by the invention of the scientific method. The *Wikipedia* entry[1] for the scientific method describes it as follows:

"The scientific method involves careful observation coupled with rigorous scepticism because cognitive assumptions can distort the interpretation of the observation. Scientific inquiry includes creating a hypothesis through inductive reasoning, testing it through experiments and statistical analysis, and adjusting or discarding the hypothesis based on the results."

One way this 'rigorous scepticism' manifests is for researchers to be suspicious of other studies and seek to recreate them to test their conclusions. This isn't easy with studies of organisations, mainly because they are all unique. Therefore, it's challenging to have a 'control' group. It's also hard to administer a placebo to some instead of an actual intervention.

The number one mantra of scientific research is that *correlation does not imply causation*. This mantra refers to the inability to legitimately deduce a cause-and-effect relationship between two events or variables solely based on an observed association or correlation between them. The idea that correlation implies causation is an example of a questionable-cause logical fallacy.

For example, the divorce rate in the US state of Maine from 2000 to 2009 had an almost perfect (99.26%) correlation with the per capita consumption of margarine[2]. When Maine residents eat more margarine, the divorce rate goes up. When they eat less, the divorce rate goes down. So, why don't we see conservative Christians advocating to ban margarine to protect family life? Because that would be silly. Despite the extremely high correlation, no evidence suggests eating more margarine makes you more likely to get divorced. Correlation does not prove causation.

Yet this same fallacy is evident in vast amounts of organisational research and many bestselling business books. In what was to become a blueprint for thousands of research efforts, in 2001, the author Jim Collins, a former McKinsey consultant, released his book *Good to Great*[3]. The book went on to sell over four million copies. According to Amazon, it is still the #3 bestselling book in the MBA Reference & Education category as of September 2024.

The *Financial Times* described the book as "...the biggest selling and most influential management book of the new millennium", with *Management Today* calling it "a must-read".

The findings in the book were held up as the outcome of five years of 'rigorous' research into the performance of 1,435 'good' companies over 40 years - finding 11 companies that became 'great'. According to Collins, the good-to-great companies averaged cumulative stock returns of 6.9 times the general market in the 15 years after their pivot to 'greatness'.

Collins claimed that the research showed that greatness could be explained by a framework that drove the differences in these 11 companies compared to the rest. The framework started with leaders with "a paradoxical blend of personal humility and professional will" who get "the right people on the bus," instil a "culture of discipline," and apply "technology accelerators." He described these elements as "the enduring physics of great organisations".

From a research perspective, several issues caused these conclusions to be later criticised by the media[4] and leading academics. Follow-up research[5] into the financial performance of the 'great' companies published in the *Academy of Management Perspectives* six years later concluded: "Only one of the 11 companies continues to exhibit superior stock market performance according to Collins' measure, and none do so when measured according to a metric based on modern portfolio theory." Collins' 'enduring physics' didn't appear to endure for very long.

A significant issue with the book and its methodology was the assertion that correlation implied causation, a cardinal sin of research. Just because a sample of successful companies shared some characteristics does not mean those characteristics caused their success. The reverse hypothesis is just as plausible. Being successful could have caused these companies to behave in similar ways.

There were other issues with the methodology. Much of the research for the book involved reading press articles (not famed for accuracy or impartiality), business school case studies (typically oversimplified and prone to bias) and financial reports (one-dimensional outputs). Interviews, although there were only 84, had leading questions and failed to consider any hindsight bias on the part of the interviewees. It was hardly surprising that managers talked about leadership, customer-centricity, values, strategic focus, etc. All of these are likely to be post-success rationalisations. They reflect the factors managers had been previously conditioned to believe caused success.

However, the most fundamental issue is the implicit assumption underlying the research, namely that the skill or capability of the leaders ultimately causes business success. Collins and his team were mainly blind to the role of luck, accidental discoveries, random interactions, unforeseen trends, unintended consequences of decisions and the myriad other possibilities of complex systems. Our rational brains tend to ignore the role of accidental success – despite the many billions of dollars generated by famously happy accidents such as the discovery of Gore-tex[6], 3M's Post-it-Notes[7], and the runaway success of Pfizer's accidental discovery[8] of the erection-forming side effects of an angina drug undergoing trials (now sold as Viagra). They did not look for much other than rational, linear explanations. They saw what they wanted to see based on the constraints of the mental models they held about how success could be achieved.

The book was targeted towards senior managers and executives, who one might expect, through higher-than-average levels of education, to have a greater chance of being exposed to concepts such as the scientific method. They should have had at least some critical thinking capability. So why did millions of them unquestioningly accept its conclusions? Let's deconstruct the appeal of Good to Great using our model of nonsense.

Step one. *Trigger aversion to uncertainty*: You [executives] don't understand how to take your companies from being good to being great. Your future is uncertain.

Step 2. *Create the illusion of sense-making*: Our 'rigorous' five years of research into over 1,400 good companies identified 11 that became great. And we know exactly how they did it: by following a framework that sets them apart.

Step 3. *Promise control over the future*: Buy this book and learn the lessons of greatness. You will understand the "enduring physics" of great companies that deliver over 6.9x the market return. And you will be able to become great, too.

It appears we can't resist this type of pseudoscience despite plenty of evidence that it's all nonsense. In his seminal 2007 book *The Halo Effect and the Eight Other Business Delusions that Deceive Managers*[9], business school professor Phil Rosenzweig takes the genre of 'success books' to task, demonstrating how poor research methodology and questionable data undermine their 'prescriptions' about how to succeed. The author of *The Black Swan*, Nassim Nicholas Taleb, described Rosenzweig's book as "one of the most important business books of all time".

In the aftermath of the global financial crisis in 2008, *Forbes* placed Rosenzweig's book at #1 on a list of *Five Must-Read Books for The Chastened CEO in 2009*, suggesting that the economic downturn had brought "even the most arrogant CEOs to their knees" and created a "potentially valuable teaching moment for those would-be masters of the universe". Unsurprisingly, the teaching moment didn't last long, and things reverted to business as usual shortly afterwards. 'Success books' continue to be the most popular genre of business books.

The Billion Dollar Secret: 20 Principles of Billionaire Wealth and Success[10] by Rafael Badziag was featured in the *Wall Street Journal*, *Forbes*, *USA Today*, on the *BBC* and in *Inc.* and *Entrepreneur* magazines. According to Badziag, the book is "based on in-depth interviews with 21 self-made billionaires" and "teaches you how to think like a billionaire and achieve amazing success in business".

Why do we believe we will be more successful if we adopt the waking-up routines, exercise regimes, reflection habits, and diets of a few billionaires? This is ridiculous on many levels. Let's take just two. Firstly, the sample size of this 'research' is tiny and not at all random (just 21 people, all chosen by the author, all billionaires) - going against all research best practices. Enlarging the sample size to thousands of randomly selected people would likely show that many far less successful people had similar routines. It would likely also show that other groups of very successful people had entirely different routines. Secondly, we come back to the questionable-cause logical fallacy. An implicit cause-and-effect assumption is at play here that has no basis in reality. Why do we think that habits are the root cause of success? What about education, background, location, network, experience, opportunity, luck, accidental discovery, being in the right place at the right time and a million other variables? It's all nonsense.

Stephen Bartlett's bestselling 2023 book, *The Diary of a CEO: The 33 Laws of Business and Life*[11], claims to have deduced a set of principles from his 'journey' and his podcast interviews that are the "fundamental laws that will ensure excellence", a "set of principles that can stand the test of time, apply to any industry, and be used by anyone who is search of building something great or becoming someone great". He modestly claims that these "laws" will work "now or 100 years from now". Sound familiar?

Maybe these books contain helpful insights, great stories and nuggets of wisdom from interesting people. And that, if nothing else, they might inspire people to have greater ambition. But we must collectively learn to question the utter nonsense of 'laws' or 'principles' that supposedly universally explain past and future success. There is no credible evidence that such things exist in a complex world.

* * *

Bias, inaccuracy and occasional fabrication of results are widespread enough in academic research. But at least in academia, to get published in a serious journal requires your research to be scrutinised by peer review. Conflicts of interest must be declared. There is a bar, even if some research sneaks under it. However, research conducted and published by the big consulting firms is not subject to the same independent challenge and review.

Remember how William Fleming of *Oxford University's Centre for Wellbeing Research* called out Deloitte for the poor quality of research underpinning their 'business case' for wellbeing? The other consultancies are no better. Accenture's 2022 report, *The CHRO as a Growth Executive*[12], claims to have found that "by activating the growth combination of data, technology and people, companies stand to gain a premium of up to 11% on top-line productivity" compared to just 4% where companies "implement data and tech solutions that fail to put people at the centre". How did they identify these 'leading companies' that 'put people at the centre'? The answer lies in the small print at the back of the report:

"Leading companies were identified by applying text analytics to earnings call transcripts...strategic focus on talent creation and digital core topics was determined through a set of keywords and phrases."

So, the 'leading' companies were chosen based on how many management buzzwords about 'talent creation' and 'digital core topics' the management team threw out in the PR-spun earnings calls with market analysts. This is not only incredibly lazy but also just plain silly.

Accenture also released a report in October 2024 titled *The Productivity Payoff: Unlock Competitiveness with Gen AI*. In the report, the authors mash up bizarrely different data sets to conclude that a new "Productivity Equation" has been validated. The equation is:

Cost Inputs x *Effectiveness Factor* x *Generative AI Multiplier*

The report concludes: "Our analysis indicates that taking a holistic approach to productivity that encompasses actions across the three dimensions could increase the productivity growth of the median company up to 16% annually", going on to suggest that "For an average-productivity performance company, this could translate to a boost of 2.8x its EBIT over a 10-year period." The three data sets mashed together to reach these conclusions were:

1. Survey data from 2,000 executives asked about "their strategies for unlocking productivity and where they invest gains." The survey results were "integrated with historical productivity trends to discern effective management practices."
2. An AI-generated analysis of 63,000 earnings calls to: "understand how leaders communicated to investors about productivity."
3. A Generative AI Labor Productivity Model "incorporating the latest findings from AI research by leading academia and AI labs, assessing the potential of generative AI to enhance both the efficiency and quality of work across various tasks."

So, let's deconstruct this odd mashup. Firstly, self-reported survey data* was examined for correlation with historical productivity trends. Once again, it appears that correlation was assumed to be causation†, given the conclusion that this allowed the authors to "discern effective management practices". This is entirely invalid from a credible research perspective. Secondly, using AI to analyse earnings calls is once more silly and lazy. All it might reveal is trends in buzzwords used on the calls, which are essentially a form of marketing. No meaningful conclusions can be drawn about actual practices in these companies. Thirdly, the assessment of the potential benefits of Generative AI was based on reviewing 25 academic experiments with no data from the actual deployment of Generative AI in the workplace. There's no evidence in the report that the results of these experiments are repeatable in real-world situations. Therefore, the actual equation in this report is:

Correlation x *Buzzword Frequency* x *Unvalidated AI Gains*

And that equals another load of meaningless drivel, frankly. Accenture should be ashamed of publishing this. If they submitted this research to any serious academic journal, the resulting hoots of laughter would resonate around academia for some time.

Another fundamental issue with consultants' research is that much of it is done in functional silos. This gives rise to 'research' that claims isolated functional interventions caused performance gains. Here are a few examples:

- *Boston Consulting Group* claims that more diverse management teams deliver a 9% higher EBIT margin than less diverse teams[13].

---

* Which any good researcher will tell you is notoriously unreliable.
† Remember the number one mantra of the scientific method: Correlation does not imply causation!

- *Accenture* claims that putting people at the centre of data and technology implementations improves "top-line productivity" by 11% (See note 7).
- *Gallup* research suggests that moving from the bottom to the top quartile on engagement delivers a median 23% uplift in profit.[14]
- *Deloitte* claims that its 2022 Digital Frontier Study[15] showed that organisations in the study with "tech savvy" boards saw, on average, 8% better year-on-year stock performance than those with "non-tech savvy boards".

Are we meant to believe these gains are entirely independent - the single root cause of significant performance improvement? This is hardly credible in a complex world. If you could increase profits from, let's say, £100m per year to £125m by adopting these recommendations, you could then invest the excess £25m in wellbeing, which, according to Deloitte, would return, on average, £117.5m. Happy days - we've more than doubled our profits... I think not. It's completely ridiculous.

Executives should view any research published by management consultants, executive coaching organisations, software vendors, and other conflicted parties with extreme scepticism. In many cases, basic research good practice is missing. Studies often focus not on random samples but on organisations cherry-picked by the authors to confirm starting hypotheses. Sample sizes are frequently too small to be statistically significant. The questionable-cause logic fallacy is endemic. Context is often completely ignored, with research findings frequently morphing into lists of the "10 top takeaways to implement in your organisation today". Don't be fooled; implementing these recommendations is invariably pointless. It will just add more silly 'stuff' to any already nonsense-strewn work landscape. Your organisation has likely already fallen for far too much of this twaddle.

It is unfortunate we can't buy many business executives for what they are worth and sell them for what they think they are worth.

-Malcolm Forbes

4

DRUNK ON THE LEADERSHIP KOOL-AID: A MODERN FAIRYTALE

Many popular leadership books push a narrative of the fairytale organisation. In the fairytale, great and modest 'servant' leaders overcome all resistance to change and magically motivate and inspire the most disgruntled workers, transforming them into model employees who deliver fantastic customer service 100% of the time. This is so far from the reality of most organisations that the bookshop category they are placed in should be *Fiction*, not *Business*.

First, we should get the bad news out of the way. There has never been or will ever be an organisation of any meaningful size where every employee loves the company, feels 'aligned to the strategy' (whatever that means), and works joyfully to achieve a perfect 10/10. Even in the most fervent cults - where members are far more emotionally invested than in a typical work setting - politics, personal agendas, and dysfunction are rife[1].

Celebrating this sugar-coated myth, there's a booming industry in American motivational corporate posters with rowers pulling together in the same direction, hands joined in teamwork, eagles soaring high and other weird proxies for organisational nirvana. For those who find this distasteful, the parody versions on sale at *www.despair.com* are far more entertaining. My favourite is the Meetings poster[2], a picture of the overlaid hands of a team. Under the image, the caption reads: "None of us is as dumb as all of us". Meanwhile, Gallup's workforce surveys[3] indicate that 51% of employees globally are looking to leave their employer. Gallup helpfully suggests crafting "inspiring values" and "living them with your employees and customers every day" might persuade them to stay. How original. Good luck with that.

Inside the organisation, the most ardent supporters of the fairytale ethos are found in Human Resources. In the years leading up to the COVID-19 pandemic, HR teams expanded like breeding rabbits in most large organisations. Teams such as *Talent Attraction, Talent Retention, Rewards & Incentives Specialists, Diversity, Equity & Inclusion, Wellbeing* and many others proliferated at terrifying speed and colossal cost. The assumption behind this industry of activity was that these factors "make us the employer of choice" (a typically meaningless aspiration), driving up employee loyalty, improving engagement, reducing attrition, and setting the organisation apart from its competition[*].

Unfortunately for the HR profession and the assumptions behind the investment in all this 'stuff', a curious side effect of the pandemic was a temporary outbreak of common sense among employees who started to realise that they had more choices. This manifested as the 'great resignation' (a catchy term invented by the media) as people took advantage of tight labour markets to jump into higher-paid roles in other companies. So much for the 'employee value proposition' and the 200 benefits.

---

[*] This being particularly amusing as every large organisation was doing exactly the same.

Just show me a little more cash, and I'll be out of here. You can keep all that other stuff.

Strangely, now that labour markets are cooling off again and people are staying put, nobody seems to be questioning why all this HR 'stuff' appeared to make no difference to loyalty or attrition. We've just carried on mindlessly as before. We don't see what we don't want to see. We still believe in the fairytale organisation. We still talk about 'getting everyone on the bus'. We still think the answer to happier employees is more internal communications and HR activity. Nobody wants to admit that even getting to a place where most employees don't actively dislike their work and all the nonsense they put up with would be an outstanding achievement.

* * *

This "Disneyfication" of work includes believing leadership is the most critical factor in organisational success. Despite decades of evidence to the contrary, we continue to believe that organisations are rational and predictable and that the 'right' leaders can reliably lead them to glory. Academics often call this belief the romantic/heroic[4] leadership theory. This belief is fundamental to maintaining the status quo. It leads to an obvious conclusion, oft-repeated like some religious mantra by overpaid recruitment consultants: "It's all about leadership," they say. And everyone nods in total agreement. Of course it is. In line with this belief, these experts rigorously assess and select leaders to find the best of the best. Invariably, many of the successful candidates are graduates of the same business schools and consulting firms we will meet shortly.

They carry the same oversimplified models of how organisations work and an unshakeable belief in their ability to solve every problem. Headhunters will point to their favoured candidate's successful career to date. The implicit assumption is that the individual's leadership qualities - not the context or serendipity - led to success. In their world, past performance is seen as a guarantee of future success. The media is equally complicit in this story, ascribing the entire success or failure of global companies to a single individual, the CEO. It's as if the many thousands of other employees in the company are irrelevant, their roles (for good or bad) in the story discounted en masse. The future rests entirely on one person. We repeatedly see this bias in leadership research. For example, research published in 2020 by the Boston Consulting Group's Henderson Institute[5] claims that by studying the tenures of 7,000 CEOs worldwide, they could "identify how much and how they affected their companies' performance trajectories." Factors for 'year' and 'industry' were controlled for (somehow). However, the primary bias remains that the performance outcomes of the entire organisation were caused by the CEO alone. It's ridiculous when you stop to think about it.

If we wanted to test the 'it's all about the leader' hypothesis, we would ideally choose a group of companies competing in an environment with as many controlled variables as possible, leaving just the leader and the context (in this case, the unique characteristics of the organisational 'system'). Luckily, we have one such environment: the English Premier League, the most-watched football league in the world. The 'beautiful game' rules rarely change. The pitch dimensions are prescribed, and the goalposts literally never move. A maximum of 11 players per team are allowed to play at any one time. Independent referees and video surveillance punish breaking the rules on the field in real time, making it difficult to win by cheating. Opportunities for innovation in the playing of the game are virtually non-existent. Players can't use any assistive technology besides football boots and hair gel. Any moves or formations one team formulates are easily and swiftly copied. Artificial intelligence can't play football for you. It's the closest thing to a controlled environment we have.

In football, as in the broader world of work, the cult of the heroic leader is alive and well. Successes and failures are laid at the feet of the managers, who receive CEO-like pay and God-like adulation (on the way up, at least). With very few exceptions, the only way to become a Premier League manager is to have a successful track record of leading other clubs from this or similar leagues to trophies. If the manager's skill was the primary cause of success, then in theory, transferring the 'successful' manager into the different organisational context of another football club should produce the same glory.

It would not appear to be so. By April 2023, 13 of the 20 English Premier League clubs had parted way with their managers in just one season. Only one (Graham Potter at Brighton) left of their own accord - an astonishing 60% failure rate. In 2012, the average tenure of a Premier League manager was just over four years. By 2022, it had dropped to two years. In any other branch of research, you would have to conclude that there was little evidence to support this hypothesis that future success was highly correlated with the previous track record of newly appointed managers. But where are the headlines about context being more critical than the last success? Despite the overwhelming evidence, we still believe that the heroic 'proven manager' model will deliver future success based on past performance.

The same shocking failure rate is at work in the wider corporate world. In 2017, research from the *Corporate Executive Board* (now part of Gartner) estimated that 50% to 70% of executives fail within the first 18 months in a new role, regardless of whether they were promoted from inside the business or recruited as an external hire[6]. It turns out context trumps the illusion of responsibility for past success.

The failure to consider context is undoubtedly made worse by the ridiculous obsession with new CEOs producing a '100-day plan'* as soon as they get their key to the executive bathroom. Boston Consulting Group offers this sage advice to new leaders[7]: "In their first 100 days, CEOs should create a multifaceted and integrated narrative that lays out their strategic ambition as well as their transformation, stakeholder management, communications, and talent assessment plans." All this in just 100 days, with little context or even knowledge in many cases. It's patently ridiculous and clearly composed by someone who's never run a company. No wonder the failure rate is so high.

Why do we not question this strange but widely held belief that one individual should be expected, or even allowed, to run a 100-day process that could - with the benefit of minimal context - decide the long-term future of the company? Is it any wonder that so many new CEOs fail? These failures come at a high cost to the organisation and individuals (mainly in middle management) who have to deal with the fallout and flip-flopping every two to three years.

Despite the high failure rates, a vast industry of leadership development and executive coaching feeds at the altar of this strange leader worship. Amazon currently features over 50,000 books on leadership. A quick search on LinkedIn shows that over 52,000 people advertise their leadership and executive

---

* The concept of a 100-day plan can be traced back to US President Franklin D. Roosevelt, who, in his 'fireside chat' to the nation in July 1933, reflected on his administration's progress in the first 100 days in office. Since then, governments and corporations have adopted the yardstick of 100 days to measure meaningful progress. It's now a default expectation for new leaders despite being silly and dangerous.

coaching expertise in the UK alone*. The need for this giant population is puzzling because we've had 80 or so years since the birth of the modern organisation to study leadership. We should have figured it out by now. How hard can it be?

This obsession has been incredibly lucrative for the 'special ones' chosen to lead large organisations. In 2023, four CEOs of US publicly traded companies were paid over $150m each, while the median CEO pay for the top 100 companies was over $29m[8]. The average American worker's compensation in 2023 was $65,470[9], meaning the average worker would have to put in 445 years to earn one year's CEO pay.

In the journal *Leadership*[10], researcher Nancy Harding reflects on the strange paradox of leaders who "hold decision-making power over more and more issues, about which they often know less and less". She observes that leaders must trust the people they lead to deliver while "simultaneously managing systems of surveillance that implicitly assume subordinates cannot be trusted."

And there is a massive elephant in the corner. If leadership is the highest-order solution, the primary lever of change, why are so many organisations so unbelievably and disappointingly mediocre? Most are a million miles away from delivering a customer or employee experience the CEO would genuinely be proud of, despite how it's dressed up in the glossy annual report. Many have a large cohort of employees who feel little natural affinity and would gladly jump ship for a relatively small pay rise (as we saw post-pandemic in a hot labour market). Extensive research shows that almost all fail to deliver the benefits they set

---

* To give a sense of scale, according to *The Health Foundation*, less than 47,000 doctors (General Practitioners) worked in the National Health Service in England in October 2023. I'll let you decide which of these populations is more beneficial to society.

out for ambitious transformation programmes[11], cultural change initiatives[12], or mergers and acquisitions[13].

Hardly a day goes by without another outrageous corporate scandal emerging. Yet nobody questions the belief. Faced with the same problems that have dogged the organisation, sometimes for decades, the default answer is to change the leader (again). Strangely, the headhunters who recommended the failed leader are never subjected to fee clawbacks. Rather than having to shoulder their responsibility for selling the flawed dream, they are given another lucrative assignment to find a replacement. Nobody seems to see the irony. When the leader fails, we blame the leader, not the system.

What happens next is entirely predictable. Under heavy expectations, the new leader will bizarrely propose broadly the same solutions as those that ultimately failed their predecessors. Typically, these will take the form of a 100-day plan based on a pick'n'mix bundle of the 'standard' responses:

- *Define and build a culture of high performance.*
- *Redefine our purpose.*
- *Address leadership capability across the business.*
- *Change our structure to align with our strategy.*
- *Get our people to really live our values.*
- *Put customers at the heart of everything we do.*
- *Drive accountability throughout the organisation.*
- *Change our incentives to drive performance.*
- *Break down silos to improve collaboration.*
- *Adopt agile ways of working across the business.*

Blah, blah, blah. The same old crap every time. It's all so dull and predictable. You hand over all that money in superstar CEO pay packages and don't even get one original thought. So fucking disappointing.

Each time, an avalanche of well-intentioned but ultimately futile endeavours kicks off, often requiring many new hires in Human Resources and Internal Communications (support functions that exist primarily to generate and propagate nonsense). This results in more 'stuff' raining down on already stressed and overburdened middle managers, pulling them away from doing something worthwhile that might improve things for customers and employees. Each time, the longest-serving frontline employees will recall that something very similar was tried before by several other since-departed leaders and made little or no difference.

With great regularity, the interventions fail to deliver the promised outcomes and will often create a raft of unforeseen consequences that worsen an already bad situation. And like members of *The Seekers* when the spaceship failed to arrive on the predicted day - instead of questioning our beliefs, we look for some other explanation for why things didn't quite work out as planned.

It was the culture. It was the communications. It was poor change management. It was the lack of middle management capability, etc. We never question the fundamental belief that leaders can predict and control the future. That would be a massive challenge to our collective belief system, to many leaders' egos, and to the highly profitable industries that support the cult of leadership, such as headhunters, business schools, leadership institutes, and executive coaches. What would they all do if enough people saw that the emperor wasn't wearing any clothes?

Here is a contrarian idea. On the appointment of a new CEO, the board should make it clear that - unless there is an unforeseen crisis - there will be no significant organisational changes for six to twelve months until the new CEO has spent enough time to properly understand the current context before developing and testing any hypotheses about the future. Imagine the relief of middle management! They could finally finish and embed some changes and enjoy a period of calm where the organisation could focus on the customer and not on itself. Crazy, I know.

All you need in this life is ignorance and confidence; then success is sure.

— MARK TWAIN

5

——————

PRETENDING IT'S ALL
RATIONAL: THE MBA GOGGLES

Harvard Business School was founded in 1908, establishing the world's first MBA programme[1] and becoming the model for business schools worldwide. In 1924, the 'case study' was adopted as the 'primary method of instruction'. This was in line with the school's aims, described in a memorandum by the Dean, Wallace Brett Donham. The aims included "giving the student training for practice in dealing with business problems". In Dean Donham's view, this was best done by practice in:

1. *Ascertaining facts*
2. *Appraising and sorting facts*
3. *Stating business problems in a business way*
4. *Analysing business problems*
5. *Reaching definite conclusions*
6. *Presenting such conclusions orally and in writing*

In other words, it created the illusion of understanding the past and resulted in overconfident conclusions that problems could be solved in the future. It was a perfect fit for our nonsense framework. It promised to reduce uncertainty by following a linear and logical process, swiftly leading the practitioner to the 'root cause' of any business problem, training them to reach a definitive solution, and equipping them with the persuasive skills to convince everybody they knew best. It was, essentially, a branded production process for overconfident nonsense. One that was adopted by almost all the other business schools that rapidly sprang up worldwide to emulate Harvard's stellar success in charging outrageously high fees to MBA students. Its proponents claim it "boasts a unique ability to make complex concepts accessible and develop students' leadership skills"[2].

And so, all was well in the land of leadership, with MBA graduates becoming increasingly sought after and more likely to lead large organisations. However, after the global financial crash in 2008 and a subsequent avalanche of other corporate scandals, attention began to focus on the shortcomings of business leaders and the education system that had prepared them for spectacular failure in these cases.

The Harvard case study method came under fire with accusations of contributing to a narrow, linear, amoral and overly financially oriented management philosophy. Academic criticisms included an over-reliance on "transformational models that stress the role of charismatic individuals, usually white men, in setting compelling visions to which all organisational actors are expected to subscribe"[3]. Harvard case studies described the success of Kodak in the 1980s and lauded the financial innovation at Enron. These were quickly rewritten as case studies of corporate failure when these corporations imploded.

The case study approach has also been implicated in the development of functionally centred leadership concepts that fail to foster critical thinking about business issues[4], exclude the voices of minorities[5], the poor and other stakeholders (including workers)[6] , and are fundamentally flawed by a false assumption that solutions that worked in one context are transferable to completely different contexts[7]. Perhaps the biggest problem with most MBA teaching is that it is highly rational. Like success books, it starts from a philosophical view that success comes from leadership skills. A striking amount of business success comes from serendipity—unplanned, fortunate discoveries made by chance, accident, or good luck. But that's hard to package up and sell. It is much easier to ignore the messy realities of life to pretend leadership skills are the dominant variable and that success follows skilled strategy development.

One of Harvard's most famous case studies was the story of Honda's success in redefining the US motorcycle market with huge sales of small motorcycles. The basis of the case study was a 1975 report by Boston Consulting Group for the British government. The report, titled *Strategy Alternatives for the British Motorcycle Industry*[8], claimed that the superior strategies of Japanese motorcycle manufacturers led to a collapse in the US market share for British motorcycle exports. BCG's report and the HBS case study that followed highlighted Honda's strategy to market small automatic motorcycles to members of the public who were not motorcyclists and had never thought about buying a motorcycle. Honda's success was positioned as a classic low-cost differentiator strategically entering a new market.

However, in a 1984 article entitled *Perspectives on Strategy: The Real Story Behind Honda's Success*[9], researcher Richard T. Pascale describes how the true story emerged when he gathered together the six executives who had led the US expansion of Honda. What emerged was a tale of mistakes, serendipity and unexpected events that blew a hole in the post-rationalised and biased BCG report and HBS case study. The now-retired Honda executives described how they had no strategy other than to aim for an arbitrarily chosen ten per cent of the market share of European motorcycle exports to the US (a target of 6,000 units per year). They set off for the US with an inventory of motorcycles, split evenly across their four models - the 50cc Supercub and the 125cc, 250cc & 305cc motorcycles. Soichiro Honda, Honda's founder, was particularly confident that the 250cc and 305cc motorcycles would do well, mainly because the handlebar shape of the larger models looked like the Buddha's eyebrows, which he took as a good omen.

When they arrived in the US, they only had enough funds to rent a one-bedroom apartment and a run-down warehouse in a poor area of Los Angeles. They were unaware of the seasonal nature of motorcycle sales in the US and arrived at the end of that year's season, finding themselves with no prospect of sales until the following year. By 1960, they had persuaded around 40 motorcycle dealers to stock some Honda motorcycles, and some of the bigger motorcycles had started to sell. But then disaster struck as dealers began to report mechanical failures. It turned out that motorcycles in the US were driven much further and faster than in Japan. Honda's engineering teams scrambled to redesign gaskets and clutches to fix the issues.

Meanwhile, the Los Angeles Honda team hesitated to move the smaller Supercub models for fear of compromising the brand's image with 'real' bikers. To conserve cash, they rode the Supercubs around LA themselves on errands and to meetings. This generated a lot of interest from bystanders who were curious about these quirky vehicles. A buyer from Sears tracked them down and tried to persuade them to sell the Supercub via the Sears catalogue, but they initially resisted. However, with sales of larger motorcycles on hold pending technical fixes, they had no choice but to push out the smaller model. Much to their surprise, the retailers who wanted to sell the Supercub were not motorcycle dealers but sporting goods retailers. Unexpectedly, the buyers were mainly ordinary non-motorcyclists, but the Honda team were reluctant to advertise to this audience in case the message impacted sales of the higher margin 'real' motorcycles.

In 1963, a student studying advertising at UCLA submitted a routine course assignment in which he had devised an advertising campaign for Honda with the slogan: *You Meet The Nicest People on a Honda.* Encouraged by the course instructor, the student showed his work to a contact at Grey Advertising who was pitching for the Honda account. Grey quickly bought the idea and showed it to Honda. The rest is history. Far from setting out with a strategy to 'redefine' the US motorcycle market - the Honda team reluctantly backed into the opportunity when serendipity presented it.

Despite extensive criticism, the case study method remains the primary teaching method at Harvard and most other business schools globally. Harvard even sells business cases to other business schools, with sales of over fifteen million copies per year, generating hundreds of millions of dollars. As a result, business schools worldwide churn out armies of MBA graduates wedded to the 'heroic' model of the individual leader who confidently guides their business to success by applying the lessons of their MBA training to the real world. Belief perseverance looks set to keep it that way.

Prominent management thinkers, including Henry Mintzberg, Professor of Management Studies at McGill University, have called for the MBA to be scrapped altogether. In Mintzberg's view, the idea of a 'foundational' education at the beginning of a manager's career is fundamentally flawed, as he believes that management is a practice that can only be learned by actually managing - not by debating case studies in a classroom. He also points out that the MBA gives graduates a falsely inflated sense of their capabilities, which can cause "tremendous harm" to organisations.

In an article titled *The Buck Stops (and Starts) at Business School*[10], Joel Podolny (Dean of Apple University & former Dean of Yale Business School) suggests that the problems with MBA education are such that many people now believe business schools are harmful to society, churning out self-interested, unethical and overly financially oriented graduates. He is also critical of the highly rational approach to MBA teaching, pointing out that business school faculty members who specialise in quantitative methods and spreadsheet models hugely outnumber those who focus on qualitative and inductive approaches.

Despite extensive criticism, the MBA remains a highly coveted 'badge'- a branded endorsement that means business school graduates get more senior roles with more power, where the impact of poor thinking and bad decisions is far more costly. Research from the *US Graduate Management Admission Council's* survey of corporate recruiters in the US[11] shows that the median starting salary for MBA graduates in 2024 was $120k, whereas the median starting salary for experienced industry hires without an MBA was $90k.

Organisations will pay over 30% more for the badge, but there's no evidence that it's worth it in terms of results. If the many criticisms of this type of education are valid, it may ultimately be detrimental to those organisations' futures.

The market for nonsense is infinite.

— JAMES RAANDI

6

THE FAD FACTORY: MANAGEMENT
CONSULTANTS' REAL WORK

Around the same time Harvard adopted the case study method, the management consulting industry was becoming established. Following the great financial crash of 1929, the Glass-Steagall Banking Act of 1933 ended the active involvement of US commercial banks in 'non-banking' activities such as business restructuring and consulting.

This new law triggered a rapid increase in demand for external advice in finance, management, and strategy. McKinsey, Booz Allen Hamilton, and a handful of other consulting firms saw rapid growth. McKinsey was one of the first firms to realise the power of pseudo-research, pioneering extensive surveys of US executives that led to lucrative contracts with the most prominent companies of the time.

Boston Consulting Group (BCG) arrived in the 1960s, founded by the charismatic Bruce Henderson[1], a former Harvard Business School graduate. Bruce understood the appeal to executives of oversimplifying a complex world, popularising the famous *BCG matrix*, a 2 x 2 grid model with market share on one axis and market growth on another. The quadrants were memorably named *problem children*, *stars*, *cash cows* and *dogs*, no doubt helping the matrix to become widely discussed and adopted and helping BCG to generate billions in sales.

Not to be outdone, McKinsey later developed its most popular over-simplification, the *7S-Framework*[2], based on the research of former McKinsey consultants Thomas J. Peters and Robert H. Waterman, who wrote the bestselling book *In Search of Excellence*[3], an early example of the success genre. 'Shared Values' were at the model's centre, which should immediately raise a red flag for any sensible observer.

Despite multiple recent scandals, most notably at McKinsey*[,4], most executives worldwide pay close attention to the opinions, insights, and research of the big consulting firms. After all, many of them were management consultants earlier in their careers. A 2008 study by USA Today calculated that the odds of a McKinsey consultant becoming CEO of a public company were the best in the world, at 1 in 690. The closest rival was Deloitte, at 1 in 2,150.

In recent years, big consulting firms have stumbled on an incredibly lucrative business development approach. Often combining reverse-justified case studies with business school articles and 'discoveries' from the bestselling books of leadership gurus, consulting firms create management fads that they hype up as rapidly as possible. They then sell their 'expertise' in the fad to executives afraid they'll miss the next big thing. To return to our nonsense framework, what they are experts in doing is:

1. *Triggering our aversion to uncertainty*
2. *Creating the illusion of sense-making*

---

* Currently under criminal investigation into its work for opioid firms, after already paying out nearly $1bn to settle civil claims that their advice fuelled America's addiction epidemic.

3. *Promising control over the future*

Fads that have burned brightly and disappeared just as quickly, generating billions of dollars in consulting revenue, have included Lean, Six Sigma, then Lean Six Sigma, Business Process Reengineering, Outsourcing, Onshoring, Delayering, Rightsizing, Agile, etc. More recently, top fads hyped by the big consulting firms have included Blockchain, Non-fungible Tokens (NFTs), Cryptocurrencies, and the Metaverse.

Deloitte's April 2022 report, *A Whole New World? Exploring the Metaverse and What it Could Mean for You*[5] aimed to "provide a brief overview of future possibilities (and pitfalls) as executives consider their entry into what some believe could be the next new world for almost every business." The report went on to suggest that the metaverse may be "a paradigm shift for consumer and enterprise behaviour" that was "analogous to the introduction of smartphones" and could create a "potentially massive new market" with estimates of commercial opportunity "as high as $13 trillion, and 5 billion regular users by 2030". According to the report, the metaverse could "reorder the competitive landscape in many industries".

Hot on Deloitte's heels, McKinsey issued their report in June 2022 entitled *Value Creation in the Metaverse: The Real Business of the Virtual World*[6], with the aim of helping "leaders of both consumer and business-to-business clients better understand its power and potential" and "identify strategic imperatives". The report stated that McKinsey's "bottom-up view" of use cases suggested that the metaverse may "generate up to $5 trillion in impact by 2030", equivalent, they said, to the entire economy of Japan. The concluding remarks even suggested that by 2030, it was "entirely plausible" that more than 50% of live events could be held in the metaverse, and more than 80% of commerce would be impacted by consumer activity in the metaverse.

Executives worldwide went into panic mode as they scrambled to try and understand how not to lose out on the multi-trillion-dollar opportunity that seemed to be materialising out of (literally) nowhere. The consultants were selling advice so quickly that they started to run out of capacity. By November 2022, the BBC reported that nearly $2bn had been spent on virtual real estate in the metaverse[7], with Samsung, UPS and Sotheby's among the companies buying land and building shops in Decentraland[8] (a leading metaverse 'world') while Adidas, Warner Music and Gucci had set up in The Sandbox[9] (seen as the leading other 'world' contender). Facebook even changed its name to Meta and announced plans to invest $10bn in Facebook Reality Labs, its metaverse division working on 'Augmented Reality' and 'Virtual Reality' hardware, software, and content[10].

So, how did it all work out? By August 2024, Meta had burned through a staggering $45 billion with little to show (reported revenues of just $2 billion in 2023). Many observers expect Meta to pull the plug on Facebook Reality Labs, given that the latest fad of Generative Artificial Intelligence has wholly pushed the metaverse out of everybody's mind. Google searches for "the metaverse" spiked in January 2022, declining steeply since then, and are currently (August 2024) averaging between 1% and 6% of their 2022 peak levels[11].

Things are not going well in Decentraland or The Sandbox, either. DappRadar (dappradar.com) provides data on transactions in the metaverse. When I last looked, on August 13th 2024, there were 374 transactions by 219 users totalling $111.31 in Decentraland. Yes, just over 100 dollars in 24 hours. In The Sandbox that day, there were 461 transactions totalling $79k. At that combined revenue generation rate, it would take approximately 173,157 years to hit $5tn. The value of virtual real estate in the metaverse has plunged, with 'land' prices in Decentraland down 95% from their peak by August 2024 and The Sandbox dropping by 89%[12]. Is the metaverse dead?* Perhaps, like the famous Monty Python parrot sketch[13], it's just 'resting'.

The sound of silence from the big consultancies about the failure of the $13tn metaverse to change everything is deafening. No refunds appear to be on offer. But no matter. They quickly found an even better fad to hype – AI. Sensing the fee-earning bonanza of a lifetime, consulting firms have latched on to the rise in Artificial Intelligence investment by the big technology firms, launching AI institutes and practices and, in some cases (e.g., PWC in the UK), announcing restructures of their organisations to meet the upcoming booming AI market demand.

In McKinsey's June 2023 report, *The Economic Potential of Generative AI: The Next Productivity Frontier*, the consultancy claimed that "Generative AI will have a significant impact across all industry sectors", suggesting that in banking alone, the technology could deliver "value equal to an additional $200 billion to $340 billion annually". The report indicates that McKinsey's "updated scenarios" now lead to estimates that "half of today's work activities could be automated between 2030 and 2060." Are you beginning to spot a familiar pattern?

Meanwhile, over at Deloitte, a new Generative AI practice was established in 2023 along with the Deloitte AI Institute. Dan Helfrich, Chairman and CEO of Deloitte Consulting, had this to say: "It's our responsibility as a society, and our responsibility as business leaders to create new talent with AI skills - not only for the engineers and data scientists but also for every single role in an organisation, no matter how technical." Every single role in

---

* I hope it is dead. The vision of a dystopian future where we all but abandon the real world to live through digital avatars with little genuine human contact is the stuff of my nightmares. The big technology companies already have far too much control and influence over our lives. Let's not let them take the rest.

every single organisation – sounds like a gold rush for the next few years, Dan. Happy days!

In a recent article titled "The A.I. Boom Has an Unlikely Early Winner: Wonky Consultants", *The New York Times* suggested that management consultants were currently the only winners from the vast investments by technology firms in AI, estimating that up to 40% of McKinsey's 2024 revenues would be from AI-related consulting - no wonder they aren't saying much about the metaverse anymore. Don't look over there; look over here. The fad factory has a shiny new product - more on AI in Part IV.

Nonsense, when earnest, is impressive, and sometimes takes you in. If you are in a hurry, you occasionally mistake it for sense.

— BENJAMIN DISRAELI

7

NOT THE MESSIAH: SIMON SINEK & THE SOUNDBITE SELLERS

I n my view, even more suspect than the genre of success books is the rise of the self-appointed 'leadership gurus' whose simplistic soundbites are slavishly accepted as genius by their millions of adoring fans. What sets the self-appointed guru apart from the success genre author is that at least many authors of success books made some attempt to back up their theories with research. In contrast, gurus convince us that their dazzling insights alone should change how we view the world. But they are not messiahs[*].

Simon Sinek's TEDx talk from 14 years ago[1] has been viewed over 60 million times. In it, he introduces the concept behind his bestselling book *Start With Why*[2]. The central idea in the book is a simplistic representation that claims to explain why some companies are wildly successful, and some are not. It's a diagram with three concentric rings, the inner titled 'why', the middle 'who' and the outer 'what'. In the talk, Simon introduces the model by claiming to have made a "discovery" that "All the

---

[*] Monty Python fans reading this will mentally finish the sentence "He's not the messiah..." (from *The Life of Brian*).

great and inspiring leaders and companies in the world...they all think, act and communicate the exact same way, and it's the complete opposite to everybody else."

Note the interesting use of language here. This is an example of 'extreme' or 'absolute' language. It leaves no space for exceptions or nuance. *All* of them, the *exact* the same way, *completely opposite* to *everybody* else. This is a ludicrous claim. It would only take one single inspiring person or company anywhere in the world not to think, act, or communicate in this "exact same way" to disprove it. However, as a rhetorical device, the extreme level of confidence pulls in the viewer or reader in the same way as claims to have decoded the 'laws' of becoming a billionaire. Somehow, the appeal of fake certainty is so hypnotic it completely bypasses our bullshit filters.

Simon's real discovery was that he could use the techniques he learned from working in New York advertising agencies to convince people that his content-light soundbites were profound wisdom. On his website (simonsinek.com), an online course called *The Art of Presenting* promises to share Simon's "secrets to captivate your audience with confidence." He is very good at that.

Simon and other gurus have learned to tap into our innate and frankly bizarre desire for organisations to resemble Disney movies, where the courageous, authentic, conscious, servant leader (who 'eats last', according to Simon's other book) is thrust reluctantly into a leadership role and creates a magical culture, turning every disengaged employee into a beautiful high performing swan and every disgruntled customer into a diehard lifelong fan. The classic hero's journey[3] played out in the office.

The gurus don't seem to see the irony of holding up Apple as an inspirational 'purpose-led' company while ignoring that Steve Jobs' leadership style was a million miles away from the mythical Disney leadership style they promote. In Walter Isaacson's Jobs biography, Joanna Hoffman (Apple employee #5) described Jobs' "uncanny capacity to know what your weak point is, to make you feel small". I'm not sure this matches Simon's assertion that leadership is not about "being in charge" but "taking care of those in your charge".

The gurus often hail Elon Musk as a visionary leader. Over at Twitter (now X), the San Francisco Department of Building Inspection announced in 2023[4] that it was investigating allegations from ex-employees that Musk had illegally turned offices into bedrooms for tired employees after telling staff they had to commit to "working long hours with high intensity" or leave. Musk responded to the investigation report on Twitter, saying the city "attacks companies providing beds for tired employees". I guess it's all OK as long as Elon had breakfast last in the morning - am I right Simon?

Other sage advice from Simon includes the assertion that "your customers will never love your company unless your employees love it first", another excellent example of absolute nonsense disguised in extreme language. He offers no evidence to support this assertion; just one example is sufficient to debunk this twaddle.

Amazon consistently scores highly on brand perception, trust and satisfaction. The 2024 *Newsweek's Most Trusted Companies in America* survey[5] ranked Amazon #2 in the retail sector. According to researchers at Qualtrix[6], Amazon had the highest brand loyalty of any US consumer company from 2019 to 2021, being nudged to a close second place in 2022/3 by Apple. Amazon's customers have a lot of love for the brand. However, plenty of evidence suggests that Amazon's employees don't feel the same love towards the company as its customers, particularly in their warehouses.

Four prominent US senators wrote an open letter[7] to Jeff Bezos in October 2020 expressing concerns that Amazon had "decided to heavily invest in systems to retaliate against freedom of expression about unsafe and unhealthy working conditions". France's data protection agency CNIL fined the company €32m in 2024 for "excessive" surveillance of its workers. The California Department of Industrial Relations recently issued fines of $5.9m to Amazon, alleging the company worked warehouse employees so hard that it risked their safety. Amazon has also been fined by the US Department of Labor, which alleged that the company failed to keep workers safe at several operational sites. Amazon disagrees with all the allegations.

The success of *Start With Why* and the millions of YouTube views generated a flurry of corporate activity worldwide. Executives who had read the book or watched the talk were determined to suddenly be 'purpose-led', even though their organisations had survived pretty well without purpose statements since they were founded. Many of these efforts ended in complete farce, with laughable purpose statements that bore no resemblance to how the company behaved (see Chapter 11 - Meaningless abstractions: vision, purpose, and values).

When leadership gurus speak, you can generally be sure that anything following the words "Leadership is all about..." is entirely vacuous. One of the things leadership perhaps should be about is having the critical thinking capability to not take this unsubstantiated, over-simplistic drivel as fact – and most definitely not to use it as the basis for launching more idiotic activity at long-suffering employees.

8
____

SELF-PROMOTING ECHO CHAMBERS: THE LINKEDIN EFFECT

Social media has accelerated the waves of idiocy hitting our organisations. Now every moron has a platform. Anyone can claim to be a 'leadership guru' or a 'culture change expert', and the algorithms create echo chambers to reinforce our misguided beliefs about organisational life.

LinkedIn, the leading platform for work-related nonsense, is awash with daily idiotic posts with titles like: "The Top Ten Things Great Leaders Do". Invariably, this content has no credible foundation; it's just click-bait for the dopamine of 'likes', the illusion of social validation and the hope that 'followers' can be monetised somehow. Each post gets liked by hundreds or even thousands of people robotically accepting this complete drivel as if it were great wisdom handed down by venerable sages on stone tablets.

Occasionally, I comment, suggesting that the content is entirely made up and stupid. But deep down, I know I'm wasting my time because people want to believe this rubbish is true. As we've seen, humans have evolved to dislike uncertainty and are inevitably drawn to simplistic representations of the world. What we believe to be reality is entirely constructed by our minds, a highly simplified version of the world, complete with all our biases.

Exploring this constructed reality, British filmmaker Adam Curtis released a short film in 2016 entitled *Living in an Unreal World*[1]. The film addresses various issues, from the hidden influence of global financial corporations to powerful social media algorithms' mass manipulation of our minds. In it, the narrator describes the unreal nature of work:

"You are managed with performance targets and measured outcomes. But as you sit in the glass-walled offices, you know the targets are manipulated and fake. And the managers know that you know. But you all sit there and pretend it is objective and rational."

Social media, particularly LinkedIn, amplifies all the other sources of work-related nonsense we suffer from. The deafening sound of mindless conformity drowns out the few dissenting voices or original thinkers. And there are reasons for most of us to tread carefully. Amy Edmondson is a professor at Harvard Business School, where she specialises in the study of workplace communication. She describes how we apply implicit rules to communication at work based on the fact we have what she describes as two jobs - the job we get paid for and the job of trying to look good. LinkedIn has become an online extension of the office, where risks of going against accepted wisdom are high and where challenges to nonsense can be misinterpreted in front of a vast audience. Most people won't risk posting their honest views any more than they would risk voicing dissenting opinions openly in the office. Even worse, on social media, a record of any mistakes is potentially permanent and visible to current and prospective employers. This is why exhortations to "bring your whole self to work" are hilariously misguided. Doing that would be incredibly risky for most of us. On other social media sites, people worry that their bosses might see the real them in all their messy glory. On LinkedIn, people craft their carefully staged identities specifically to be seen by bosses.

It's amusing to see how people on the platform jump on trends to try and make themselves look good. After the COVID-19 epidemic, words such as 'authenticity' and 'vulnerability' began to be used more frequently. This led to waves of highly unauthentic over-sharing, often featuring posts starting with statements such as: "I've thought long and hard about sharing this on LinkedIn but finally decided to go for it". Good for you, yawn. Writing in a blog[2] on the London School of Economics website, Shani Orgad, a Professor in the Department of Media and Communications, identifies three main 'genres' of vulnerability self-promotion posts. The first is *Triumph over Tragedy* - where posters share their vulnerabilities in the context of overcoming them, portraying themselves as resilient and motivated. These often include annoyingly cheesy quotes on self-belief. The second is *Snap*, where users focus on having reached a breaking point where they are unwilling to continue in a toxic workplace. Pictures in medical settings often accompany these posts. The image is of the brave victim courageously sharing their terrible experience. A cynic might suggest that this could be a handy way to explain being fired. The third is *Subversive Commentary on Self-Promotion*. These posts usually use subversive language to parody the overwhelming tendency of LinkedIn users to promote themselves constantly. These often start with introductions like: "I'm thrilled to announce," followed by news of being laid off or rejected for multiple roles. Orgad says, "Vulnerability has become an iteration of digital self-promotion. Vulnerability posts tend to attract attention, likes, shares and comments, and are consequently promoted by LinkedIn's algorithm."

One of the most notorious vulnerability posts on LinkedIn went viral in 2022[3] when marketing company CEO Braden

Wallace shared a selfie showing him crying after making two members of staff redundant. "This will be the most vulnerable thing I'll ever share," he wrote before going on to make it all about him. The first comment on his post was a single word: Muppet. The platform's users quickly dubbed him "The Crying CEO". Wallace became the poster boy for what behavioural insights expert Helen Jambunathan[4] calls the "LinkedIn cringe". Thankfully, some people on LinkedIn use this nonsense for comedy value. I particularly like this post from Andrew Tobin[*], a US-based Creative Director:

My 4-year old froze on stage at her first ballet recital.

"I failed" she told me after the show.

I looked at her heartbroken, with tears in my eyes.

"No. I failed you. But today, you've given me more than I could've ever asked for. You gave me a sad kid story to post on LinkedIn."

"Link what?" she asked.

"LinkedIn", I replied. "A place where depressing personal anecdotes involving imaginary children are posted and mined for engagements in order to boost one's own professional identity."

She looked at me, confused.

"But dad–"

I cut her off.

"Shhhh."

Social media platforms have their uses, but we must collectively become more aware of their dark sides. The short-form content and algorithms feed on our love of over-simplification and create the veneer of credibility from the social currency of likes. It simply reinforces existing belief systems. Most of the content is self-promotion in disguise. This is not the wisdom of the crowd; it's the complete opposite. You won't find it here if you seek genuinely disruptive ideas or innovation. A far better

---

[*] https://www.linkedin.com/in/andrewjtobin/

option would be to travel, meet new people and explore what interesting companies are doing in sectors that are very different from yours. Something about a marked change in an environment seems to get the creative juices flowing.

PART II

LOOKING FOR ANSWERS IN ALL THE WRONG PLACES

The uncreative mind can spot wrong answers, but it takes a very creative mind to spot wrong questions.

— ANTONY JAY

9
———

MODERN-DAY WITCHCRAFT: CORPORATE CULTURE

Diane Purkiss is a Professor of English Literature at the University of Oxford and an expert in witchcraft beliefs and their representation in popular culture. In a fascinating interview for *English Heritage*[1], she describes how witches and witchcraft became part of popular culture in England.

One of the factors she identifies is the preoccupation of 12th - 14th-century monasteries with the moral dilemma presented by the monks' wet dreams. Fearful of being considered sinful, monks reported that their nocturnal adventures often resulted from being straddled in their sleep by a mysterious female figure. As no women were allowed in the monastery, it seemed reasonable to conclude that the intruders must be witches - devils taking the form of females to tempt monks into sexual sin.

By the 17th century, the fear of witches was widespread, leading to professional witch hunters roaming the land, the most notorious being Matthew Hopkins, who wrote a book about his witch hunting called *The Discovery of Witches*. In his 3-year quest, Hopkins sent over 300 innocent women to be hanged for witchcraft, more than the total of the previous 150 years.

Witchcraft had become the thing to blame when you couldn't understand why things went wrong, when your mental models of the world failed to provide answers, or when you needed a convenient excuse to have somebody disappear.

It was so widely accepted as real that the English Parliament passed a Witchcraft Act[*] in 1541, defining witchcraft as a crime punishable by death. A further Witchcraft Act in 1603 broadened the definitions of witchcraft and inspired Matthew Hopkins to appoint himself as 'Witchfinder General'.

Although we have largely stopped believing in witches, the world of work has a very similar construct: culture. The term 'corporate culture' was invented in the 1950s by Elliott Jaques[†,2], a Canadian psychoanalyst, social scientist and management consultant. The idea of corporate culture quickly caught on, becoming rapidly accepted as 'real' despite a complete lack of agreement among academics about what it meant and whether or not it even existed. A Rand review[3] of how social scientists define corporate culture concluded: "It is clear that the definitions of culture and corporate culture are varied and often conflicting, with no real consensus on what is meant by these terms."

We can't see or touch culture or even agree on a definition of what it is supposed to be. Still, everybody talks about it as if there is a universal understanding and acceptance of its meaning and existence. A recent survey showed that 78% of Fortune 1000 CEOs believe culture to be one of the top three factors affecting their firm's performance[4]. *Harvard Business Review* archives feature over five thousand articles discussing culture. A search on LinkedIn for the term 'culture' in job titles

---

[*] Full title: *An Act against Conjurations, Witchcrafts, Sorcery and Inchantments.*

[†] Jacques is also well known for inventing the term 'midlife crisis', another concept widely believed to be real despite a body of psychological research indicating that it's a myth.

throws up almost 2.4 million profiles worldwide (mainly HR-related roles).

Despite its largely abstract and undefined nature, culture is routinely blamed for everything that goes wrong in organisations. Every severe case of corporate or institutional malfeasance, every scandal, every case of executive greed and institutional bad behaviour - it was the culture[*].

In early 2018, after a string of high-profile corporate failures in the UK, the *Chartered Institute of Internal Auditors* warned boards to "get a grip" on "unhealthy corporate cultures" in the aftermath of a procession of what they described as "culture-related scandals". Not to be outdone, Sir John Thompson, CEO of the UK's *Financial Reporting Council*, issued the following statement: "A series of company collapses linked to unhealthy cultures - whether that be BHS, Carillion, Greensill or Patisserie Valerie - have demonstrated why cultivating a healthy culture, underpinned by the right tone from the top, is fundamental to business success." Later the same year, after the collapse of the outsourcing firm Carillion, the UK parliament issued a report decrying the "rotten corporate culture" in which executives prioritised their financial gain over employees, shareholders, and even disadvantaged schoolchildren who relied on Carillion's services for the delivery of free school meals[5]. Other enquiries have reached remarkably similar conclusions: the Volkswagen emissions scandal, culture; the Enron collapse, culture; the Wells Fargo fake accounts scandal, culture; the NASA Challenger Space Shuttle disaster, culture; and on it goes. Culture really is the new witchcraft.

After every significant UK scandal, an inquiry is convened

---

[*] My thanks to Rob Briner, Professor of Organisational Psychology at Queen Mary University London, whose insightful LinkedIn posts on this topic prompted me to dive into the research on culture.

under the leadership of some worthy former CEO or chair, now a Dame or Lord with multiple directorships. Quite why we expect these quintessential products of the system to come to a more meaningful conclusion is a mystery. Given that they've spent their entire careers benefiting from the status quo, it's hardly surprising that they stop at culture – they will never step back and take a critical look at the system in its broader sense.

"It was the culture m'Lady. The prosecution rests its case".

If we use the term culture to describe widespread bad behaviour, surely we shouldn't be so appallingly intellectually lazy as to halt our enquiries there. If culture is supposed to be unique, why are these behaviours far from unique? We see the same greed, lies, cover-ups and excessive risk-taking time after time. We see executives who seem detached from reality and the consequences of their decisions over and over. We see the perverse influence of outsized financial incentives playing out repeatedly. We see the patterns of inevitable failures of governance 'best practice'. To quote the Yankee's legendary Yogi Berra: "It's like deja vu all over again."

We can't just keep saying culture, culture, culture like a broken record every time the corporate shit hits the fan. It's ridiculous. What is this witchcraft we call culture? Do we even know culture exists? Is there any good evidence that culture affects performance and behaviour? Can it even be measured if we can't see or touch it? And how do we know whether any of the self-proclaimed culture change 'experts' and their methodologies affect organisational performance?

Luckily for those seeking answers to such questions, a landmark 2022 evidence-based review[6] by the *Center for Evidence-Based Management (CEBMa)* set out to tackle these thorny questions with a wide-ranging look at the academic literature about the link between organisational culture and performance. You may want to look away now if you are among the 92,000 people advertising their 'culture change' expertise on LinkedIn in the UK. The review findings include:

1. There's no consensus about what the term 'organisational culture' means or how it can be measured.
2. The link between organisational performance and culture is too weak to be meaningful (if it exists at all).
3. And no evidence demonstrates that interventions to change culture improve organisational performance.

The review sums it up beautifully in concluding:

"...the findings are very clear: there is little evidence consistently linking organisational culture to performance, but if such a link should exist, it is very weak and too small to be practically meaningful. As such, organisations and practitioners should be careful spending time and money on culture change programmes as they are not likely to increase performance."

Whoops. We might need a new suspect (and some other 'expertise' for those 92,000 LinkedIn profiles). Perhaps instead of blaming culture for all the bad behaviour and scandals at work, we should look for evidence of what's really causing these issues. Given the regularity and severity of corporate scandals that unfold year after year, it's reasonable to conclude that these are the tip of the iceberg. There's little reason to think that the greed, cover-ups, and abuses of power are only happening in this small subset of organisations that got caught and were, therefore, exposed.

If culture is not the culprit, something else must be at play, explaining why the patterns we see play out repeatedly. So, what factors create the conditions in which bad behaviour, stupidity and nonsense thrive, maybe not every time, but with great regularity? If culture is just a 'smoke and mirrors' distraction, there are potentially huge savings from eliminating the vast army of pointless jobs focused on culture. Could this be bigger and easier than touted savings from deploying Generative Artificial Intelligence? Food for thought. People are fond of repeating the old adage, "Culture eats strategy for breakfast". I don't think so. Next, let's look at the evidence that points to an entirely different culprit.

10

ASKING FOR TROUBLE: POWER & HIERARCHY

There's a far more compelling suspect than culture in the search for blame for corporate bad behaviour and nonsense. And that is power. Most organisations have an identical model of power distribution. Power is highly concentrated in a few individuals at the top and reduces in concentration as it travels down through the layers of middle management. When we arrive at the bottom of the hierarchy, where most employees work, they are essentially powerless.

As we saw in our brief history of modern organisations, we have long been conditioned to believe that the standard hierarchy is the only option to consider when designing organisational structures. We simply don't consider any alternatives. Most people believe this hierarchical power distribution is the 'natural' way humans have organised their collective efforts since the dawn of time. We are highly wedded to what researchers have called 'heroic leadership'[1]. However, many academics now dispute this belief, suggesting that power hierarchies may go against the very essence of human nature. For roughly the past 5,000 years, we have lived in societies dominated by the privileged few. However, egalitarian hunter-gatherer societies were the norm for 90% of human history[2]. They shared similar principles – individual autonomy, equality, sharing of resources, cooperation, and consensus-based decision-making. Most, like the Hadza people who still live an ancient nomadic lifestyle in Tanzania today, had no concept of hierarchy or laws[3].

When humans developed the technology to make agriculture feasible, there was no longer a need to be nomadic. Concepts of land ownership developed, and with them came the start of status and privilege. In the pursuit of resources and power, workers needed to be controlled for the first time, and slavery became established. In the case of the Pharaohs of Egypt, the rich became all-powerful, even declaring themselves gods. Wars broke out, with rulers seeking ever more territory and riches.

In their book *The Dawn of Everything: A New History of Humanity*[4], authors David Graeber and David Wengrow recount how ideas of 'civilised' societies emerged as a reaction to 18th-century criticism of European society by indigenous tribes in North America. In the mid-17th century, France was busy colonising large areas of what's now Canada. The Native American tribes who lived there were universally appalled at the Europeans' culture, their pursuit of greed, their lack of individual freedom, their obsession with hierarchy, and their slavish obedience to a king. They simply couldn't understand why anybody would want to live that way. They described European society as inhuman and unnatural, much to the discomfort and annoyance of the French and others.

In his memoir *Curious Dialogues with a Savage of Good Sense Who Has Travelled* (1703), French Deputy Governor-General Lahontan recalled his conversations with a statesman called Kandiaronk[5] from the Wendat tribe, who explained why his people would never adopt hierarchy or money: "Over and over I have set forth the qualities that we Wendat believe ought to define humanity – wisdom, reason, equity – and demonstrated that the existence of separate material interests knocks all these on the head."

Further south in what is now the USA, the natives were equally scathing about European society. In a letter written in 1753[6], Benjamin Franklin reflected on whether the Native American criticisms were right and whether their lifestyle was more in tune with human nature:

"When an Indian child has been brought up among us, taught our language and habituated to our customs, yet if he goes to see his relations and make one Indian ramble with them, there is no persuading him ever to return...when white persons of either sex have been taken prisoners young by the Indians, and lived a while among them, tho' ransomed by their friends, and treated with all imaginable tenderness to prevail with them to stay among the English, yet in a short time they become disgusted with our manner of life, and the care and pains that are necessary to support it, and take the first good opportunity of escaping again into the woods, from whence there is no reclaiming them."

* * *

More recent evidence suggests that we appear hard-wired to prefer egalitarian constructs. A study published in 2022 showed that children as young as six years old recognise decision-making structures and instinctively prefer group structures with shared decision-making over hierarchical group structures where a leader makes the decisions[7]. Ancient wisdom seems justified, and not for the first time. We now have an ever-increasing body of evidence showing how being handed power affects our cognitive processes, our behaviours, and our views of others. And it's not pretty.

Paul Piff runs the *Morality, Emotion & Social Hierarchy Lab* at the University of California Irvine. He and his team have spent two decades researching the effects of power, wealth and hierarchy on individuals. Paul writes: "I have been finding that increased wealth and status in society lead to increased self-focus and, in turn, decreased compassion, altruism, and ethical behaviour." A series of seven studies[8] in the field and the lab revealed that wealthier individuals behave more unethically than less wealthy individuals. They were more likely to break the law while driving, exhibit unethical decision-making tendencies, take valuable resources from others, lie in negotiations, cheat to win prizes, have more favourable attitudes toward greed, and endorse unethical behaviour at work. Next time you use a pedestrian crossing, double-check the type of car coming towards you. In one of the seven studies, researchers found that 45% of the drivers of the most expensive category of cars failed to yield to pedestrians, compared to 0% of drivers in the least costly car category.

High power is also associated with greater social distance and decreased individuation[9], resulting in those in powerful roles viewing others as less important - judging them more on their social roles than as individuals[10]. Those with more powerful roles have also been shown to express greater prejudice and stereotyping[11]. You might wonder if these descriptions apply to people who have always been in a privileged position. However, research also shows that those from a less wealthy background who make it to the top are even less sensitive to the difficulties of the less powerful than those born rich[12].

The evidence shows a strong likelihood that even if you started out pretty well-adjusted, being placed in a position of power and status will lead you to higher levels of self-interest, lower levels of compassion for others, and higher risk of behaving unethically. Non-academics might refer to this as a reasonably high risk of becoming an asshole.

But wait a minute. Are these not exactly the same executive behaviours we see repeatedly in scandal after corporate scandal, the ones we all blame on the culture...

What about the effects of being powerless at the bottom of the hierarchy? Research published in *The Journal of Applied Psychology* in 2020[13], catchily titled: This Job is (Literally) Killing Me: A moderated-mediated model linking work characteristics to mortality, found that employees' mental health and mortality were strongly correlated with the amount of autonomy they had in their jobs, their workload, and their cognitive ability to deal with the demands of the job.

"When job demands are greater than the control afforded by the job or an individual's ability to deal with those demands, there is a deterioration of their mental health and, accordingly, an increased likelihood of death" said Erik Gonzalez-Mulé, Assistant Professor of Organizational Behaviour and Human Resources at the Indiana University Kelley School of Business and the paper's lead author. On the other hand, the researchers found that job demands resulted in better physical health and a lower likelihood of death when paired with more control of work responsibilities. A lack of autonomy at work is not just stressful and depressing – it could literally kill you.

Other researchers have found that the powerless experience constraints due to a lack of personal control, increasing the potential for punishment, threat, and uncertainty[14]. This activates what's known as the Behavioural Inhibition System (BIS), which is associated with negative subjective emotions such as anxiety, fear, sadness, and frustration[15]. Rather than thinking creatively, powerless people focus on loss aversion and avoiding risk. In most organisations, the employees with the least power and autonomy are the ones we put in front of the customers. And then we wonder why high engagement, excellent service and creative thinking in frontline roles are so rare.

Meanwhile, in middle management, those in lower-powered executive roles tend to exhibit unethical behaviour when it comes to self-promotion[16], being more likely to considerably inflate their accomplishments or the importance of their role in business success. Other research on the effects of hierarchy on frontline managers[17] found that they viewed themselves as "disempowered go-betweens" stuck in the middle of conflicting demands from above and below. They tended to "compensate for their perceived lack of power in policymaking and implementation by using 'micropower' strategies to assert their power". Think David Brent from *The Office*.

Interestingly, many of these patterns of behaviour that result from hierarchies of power were observed and codified as far back as the 1960s, when Barry Oshry, a pioneering researcher and systems thinker, began a series of simulations called the *Power Lab*[18]. In the experiments, a group of strangers was immersed in a 10-day 24/7 simulation, creating hierarchies of power that led to all kinds of unexpected consequences, including, at one stage, threats of kidnap and arson as the powerless rebelled against the powerful. However, over several years of observing the experiment, Barry noticed that the same behaviour patterns kept emerging time after time, regardless of who he put in the simulation. The system, not the individual, was predictive of the behaviour.

And so, it appears that we have unwittingly defaulted to an organisational design philosophy that creates the perfect conditions for executives to become detached from reality and have little regard for the consequences of their increasingly unethical decisions; for middle management to be stuck as go-betweens, exercising 'micropower' abuse while focusing on self-promotion; for employees at the bottom to experience powerlessness, stress, burnout, depression and even premature death; and for customers to try and get good service amidst all this chaos. This is not culture. These are the unfortunate and entirely predictable consequences of hierarchies of power at work.

It gets worse. Not only does the hierarchical distribution of power create all this dysfunction, but it has also created a vast industry of nonsense that plagues our organisations and causes so much frantic activity that we never step back and examine the very nature of the systems we have created. We are too busy with the nonsense of culture, purpose, values, wellbeing, and many other completely meaningless distractions. These are the organisational equivalent of the useless nutritional supplement. Everybody is taking them, but they have no effect. We try to address the symptoms but never the underlying causes.

If power is at the heart of dysfunction and nonsense, then instead of trying to put checks and balances in place forever to mitigate the poor outcomes, why not just avoid giving people too much or too little power in the first place? Prevention is undoubtedly a better option than cure. Why are we so wedded to the extreme concentration of power in a few individuals when this is a significant factor in corporate bad behaviour? Why do we create systems that leave so many powerless when we have strong evidence of poor consequences for individuals and the organisation's performance?

The hierarchy of power might also help us understand not just how bad behaviour emerges with such lamentable regularity but also why nonsense at work is so endemic and persistent. In the rarified atmosphere of executive leadership, individuals exist in an echo chamber that reflects their already embedded beliefs. Almost 90% of *Fortune 500* CEOs are men. Many have similar educational backgrounds, with over 50% holding MBA degrees. MBA graduates comprised nearly 40% of all C-suite executives on the 2022 *Fortune 1000* list. Research by LinkedIn in 2018 looked at the first jobs listed in the profiles of those with CEO in their title. In first place: management consultant. They interact with similar leaders. They attend exclusive events organised by management consultancies and business schools. These events often feature celebrity leadership gurus evangelising on their latest theories. They are all exposed to the same fads and fashions. Leaders are no less susceptible to nonsense than the rest of us, but they are far more able to act on it on a larger scale and with more severe consequences. And the extreme level of groupthink in the echo chamber ensures that almost all organisations adopt the same practices and jump on the same fads. Power and hierarchy hold us in the nonsense doom loop. But there is a better way, as we will discover in Part V.

11

MEANINGLESS ABSTRACTIONS: VISION, PURPOSE & VALUES

Until recently, organisations were fine without vision, purpose, and values statements. However, these days, it is rare to find a large organisation without these woven throughout its internal communications and annual reports. Why does everybody do this? Because everybody else does - the usual reason for blind conformity.

The interesting thing about most vision statements is that they are not very visionary. Most describe the organisation's long-term aspirations in the language of its current business model, which would appear to rule out any significant innovation, discovery, or pivot. Nokia started as a wood pulp mill before branching into rubber tyres[1]. I'm pretty sure they didn't envision becoming a global telecoms giant (mainly because mobile phones hadn't been invented yet). Three PayPal employees founded YouTube as a video-powered dating site for helping nerds find "hook-ups". Airbnb set out to solve the accommodation needs of conference attendees. They both look somewhat different to their original visions, which were only set out a few years ago.

United Utilities has a vision to: "be the best UK water and

wastewater company". Luckily, it's not very ambitious, as most of their competitors look equally inept. However, it also assumes that the business model is suitable for the long term. I guess that saves the CEO and executive team from thinking about it. Unilever's vision is "to be the global leader in sustainable business". Why would you have a vision like that when your business model arguably makes you one of the most unsustainable businesses on the planet[*]? This implies that the top team at Unilever will continue with their strategy to stick their heads in the sand and ignore reality while carrying on with the current model for as long as they can get away with it.

If we've learned anything from the past 100 years, everything will change. Having a long-term vision doesn't make sense if you have no idea what opportunities or threats will emerge. There's an infinite number of possibilities for the future. What makes us think the one we made up on the corporate away day will be the winner? If you need a vision, why not acknowledge that you can't predict the future and frame a vision around things you could do to engage better with the future as it emerges? Examples could include:

- Increasing the chances of success through serendipity[†]. Hiring interesting people, making unorthodox connections, taking an interest in other sectors and emerging technologies, travelling to different countries - these and other things might boost your chances.
- Investing in exploring some left-field ideas your

---

[*] Unilever was the world's third leading plastic polluter, according to the 2023 Brand Audit by *Break Free From Plastic* (https://www.breakfreefromplastic.org/).
[†] Defined by the Cambridge Dictionary as "the fact of finding interesting or valuable things by chance."

teams propose, not because there's a rational
business case but because they are really interesting.

As discussed earlier in the book, Simon Sinek made the concept of 'purpose' for organisations famous in his bestselling book *Start With Why* - a great example of over-simplifying a complex world with appealing soundbites backed by biased second-hand observations. One fundamental problem with purpose statements is that - whether we like it or not - the real purpose of many corporations is to make money for their shareholders. Take the FTSE100, for instance, the UK's 100 most valuable listed companies by market capitalisation. Over 50% of shares in these 100 companies are owned by large institutional investors (pension funds, sovereign wealth funds, asset managers, etc.). Their job is to invest other people's money to generate financial returns. Higher returns attract more money, leading to higher fees. Of course, these investors would instinctively prefer to make returns by investing in companies that do good, but in a competitive world, returns come first. Their business model depends on it. This is where 'purpose' runs into problems. Unless the organisation's business model can profitably deliver the purpose, the purpose is meaningless.

Let's take some examples. Land Securities (Landsec) plc is one of the UK's largest real estate companies. When CEO Mark Allan took over at Landsec in 2020, he reframed the purpose as "Sustainable places. Connecting communities. Realising potential". Mark shifted the strategy and business model towards urban regeneration, which delivers what the purpose says. Sustainability is critical because building cutting-edge sustainable office buildings attracts a rental premium from wealthy organisations keen to showcase their environmental credentials. Regenerating an urban area creates opportunities that attract new, higher-earning residents, creating new customers for Landsec's residential, retail, and leisure developments. The purpose makes perfect sense in the context of the business model.

On the flip side of the coin lies United Utilities, the UK's most polluting water company in 2023, according to the UK's Environment Agency[2]. According to reports in *The Guardian* newspaper, one of the company's pipes spilt sewage into the River Ellen, near the Lake District, for nearly 7,000 hours in 2023. The company outraged public opinion by paying shareholders more than £300m in dividends in 2023 while operating 10 of the country's 20 most polluting water pipes. Their stated purpose:

"To provide great water for a stronger, greener and healthier Northwest".

Is this some kind of bad joke? Having worked on projects in the water industry, I can tell you that this purpose is entirely incompatible with delivering shareholder returns. Why? The business model is essentially a game because of the quirks of the UK's privatised essential infrastructure. In each round of the game, the water companies seek more funding than they need to maintain and improve the infrastructure. They then work out how to play the regulatory framework to avoid the worst penalties whilst maximising profits to distribute to shareholders. The rules change every few years as the regulator tries to stay on top of the gaming, but the water companies are better at playing the game. Bluntly, they can afford to hire smarter people. As with most regulated industries, anybody with real talent in the regulator gets poached by those regulated. With shareholder returns in complete conflict with purpose, guess which wins? The public smells something wrong - metaphorically and literally, in this case. Other water companies have now been exposed as behaving equally badly. Thames Water is on the brink of collapse as its investors play high-stakes poker with the regulator, threatening to stop funding the business unless they impose colossal price increases for customers with no alternatives. Whoever thought that privatising monopolies would end well? Muppets.

* * *

Values are even more suspect. The idea that corporate values somehow change the way people in organisations think and behave is perhaps one of the craziest unquestioned beliefs about work life. Statements like 'everybody just needs to live our values' are bandied about unchallenged as if they had some meaning. Internal communications teams create an industry of spin, reverse engineering initiatives and targets to line up under the values. HR teams create a parallel cottage industry to generate awards for 'living the values' and force the values into performance appraisal frameworks. This leaves poor middle managers to pretend that trying to assess whether employees are 'living the values' (whatever that even means) is firstly a good use of time and secondly makes any difference to how people behave. So much energy, focus, and time is wasted when other things - like delivering for the customer - continue to be predictably mediocre.

Values seem to fall into four categories. The first is the *Silly Inverse,* which contains values describing good behaviour, such as integrity, ethics, honesty, responsibility, trust, and doing the right thing. If you apply the inverse, these values become silly. For example, why would you want values of dishonesty, untrustworthiness, doing the wrong thing, etc.? The second type of value is *Delusional.* Values in this category typically reflect the kind of organisation the CEO would like to lead, not the one they actually lead - and are, therefore, broadly meaningless fantasies. This category features innovation, agility, courage, passion, creativity, etc. The plaintive hope is that by adopting these corporate values, the organisation will somehow change itself to resemble them. I was once asked to be on a 'pop-up board' of external experts convened to help the HR director of a FTSE100 business think through one of their pressing issues. Her opening statement describing the issue made me laugh aloud, attracting several disapproving glances. She said: "Innovation is one of our core values, but the problem is that we're not at all innovative." For me, that statement perfectly captures the absurdity of the delusional value.

The third category of values is *Compliance Rebadged*. In this category, companies are legally obliged to demonstrate compliance, or shareholders expect action on specific topics they view as non-negotiable. Values in this category include safety, quality, diversity, inclusion, and sustainability. Finally, the fourth and probably most meaningless category is *Basic Work Stuff*. These values tend to be included when the team making up the values runs out of ideas. This category contains values such as teamwork, collaboration, relationships, etc. - stuff that no organisation in the world could function without anyway.

The problem with espousing *Silly Inverse* values is that people, in the end, will be people. Humans became the dominant species on our planet through their ability to collaborate and build large-scale societies. Partly, that was down to language development, which allowed us to create and share stories, meanings, and ideas. However, a large part was, and still is, that most people have a decent built-in moral compass, the ability to judge right from wrong, assess their actions' impact on others, and feel a sense of empathy. A tiny minority will act in bad faith, disregard others, and maximise personal gain in ways the majority disapproves of. And as we saw in the last chapter, power is a critical factor in this deviant behaviour.

The idea that most employees who naturally behave honourably must be told to act with 'integrity' or 'do the right thing' is insulting and condescending. Do we believe that most people would behave without integrity unless it appeared in the values that adorned their company-issued coffee mugs or stress balls? Equally ridiculous is the suggestion that employees about to misbehave would somehow change their intended course of action because a values poster over the urinals encouraged them to have the highest ethical standards*. Values are the corporate equivalent of *Baby on Board* stickers, which new parents display on their back windshields in the misguided hope that seeing the sticker will magically persuade other drivers to behave better.

Here's an example of the typical type of twaddle about values featured in the Harvard Business Review article: *It's Time to Take a Fresh Look at Your Company's Values* (March 28, 2022).

"Values are the moral code of an organisation — the set of rules you all embrace and abide by that reflect the ethics of the people in the organisation and hold everyone accountable to the right standard of behaviour."

It's complete and utter rubbish. Almost every organisation where people behaved amorally or immorally had highly moral values. So, what happened? How did the values fail to uphold the proper standards of behaviour? How did this 'moral code' fail so spectacularly? Maybe they should have displayed the values posters in more toilets or handed out more values-branded stress balls. Here are just a few examples where values turned out to be entirely pointless - but the list is almost endless:

Wells Fargo Bank's values: *What's Right for Customers, Ethics, People as a Competitive Advantage, Leadership.*

Wells Fargo Bank agreed to $3bn in criminal and civil penalties for fraudulently opening millions of customer accounts without the customers' knowledge. To try to redirect the blame, the bank subsequently fired 5,300 employees. Wells Fargo did

---

* A real-world example from a construction firm I once visited.

what was wrong for the customers, acted completely unethically, used people as scapegoats and was slammed by a congressional committee for appalling leadership. A brilliant example of 'values' bullshit was contained in a 2012 document entitled *The Vision & Values of Wells Fargo*[3]. Later-to-be disgraced Chairman, President & CEO John G. Stumpf had this to say: "Corporate America is littered with the debris of companies that crafted lofty values on paper, but when put to the test, failed to live by them. We believe in values lived, not phrases memorised." Well said, John. Hilarious really.

Boeing's values: *Safety, Quality, Integrity.*

Boeing agreed to pay $2.5bn in 2021 to settle US criminal charges that it hid information from safety officials about the design of its 737 Max planes, implicated in two fatal crashes that killed 346 people. In early 2024, after a door plug blew out in flight on another Boeing aircraft, the Federal Aviation Authority (FAA) told top Boeing officials that they had 90 days to develop a plan to address: "systemic quality-control issues to meet the FAA's non-negotiable safety standards".

PWC Australia #1 Value: *Act with Integrity.*

PWC sold its lucrative government consulting business for $1 in 2023, attempting to contain a scandal in which it is accused of using secret information about government tax plans to make millions in fees from advising multinational companies on how to avoid the upcoming tax changes. This complete failure to act with integrity has led to the departure of the PWC Australia CEO and seven other senior partners, and criminal investigations are ongoing.

Ernst & Young #1 Value: *[People who] Act with integrity*

EY was hit with a record $100 million fine by the US government in 2022 after regulators discovered that the company knew some of its auditors were cheating on exams for several years and did nothing to stop it. The Securities Exchange Commission noted: "The SEC will not tolerate integrity failures by independent auditors who choose the easier wrong over the harder right."

Delusional values are equally problematic because most organisations are inherently set up to defeat any attempts to resemble them. Take innovation, for example. CEOs are concerned about a lack of innovation in their organisations. One recent survey of global CEOs[4] shows that 45% think their organisation will no longer be economically viable in 10 years if it continues on its current trajectory. But why not make innovation a core value and get everyone to 'live it'? Job done.

Or maybe it's not that simple. Do you want all your employees 'living' innovation – or do you want most of them to do their day job well and to think about improvements occasionally? You might be better off focusing most of the organisation on doing the basic stuff well - like meeting your customers' by now low expectations (unless one of your values was *customer service*, in which case everything is undoubtedly fine).

This is why Lockheed originally developed the concept of 'skunk works' innovation - where you have a few highly creative and skilled individuals 'living' innovation, wholly separated from the rest of the organisation. In 1943, Lockheed Chief Research Engineer Kelly Johnson enlisted an elite team of engineers and mechanics to build a new aeroplane prototype under strict secrecy and a seemingly impossible deadline. One hundred and forty-three days later, America's first fighter jet, the XP-80 Lulu Belle, rolled out of Lockheed's Burbank, California facility. In the 80 years of skunk works since, innovations include the 1950s U2 spy plane that flew to the edge of space to avoid Russian radar (and is still flying today), the 1960s SR-71 Blackbird (still the fastest and highest-flying aircraft ever made), the first pilotless aerial system (or drone), the stealth fighters and bombers of the 1970s & 1980s and the X-35 fighter prototype that paved the way for the modern F-35 fighter aircraft. Many other organisations have successfully adopted this concept[5].

And what do 'courage' and 'bravery' even mean in the office? Very few organisations are fighting a war or putting their employees in grave danger (apart from some shady private security outfits). Wouldn't a brave CEO at United Utilities scrap the dividend and the executive bonus scheme to pay for fixing leaking sewage pipes that are causing substantial environmental damage? After all, 'doing the right thing' is one of their core values...

12

LAZY AND INFANTILISING: THE ENGAGEMENT SURVEY

Like many facets of modern work life, employee surveys can be traced back to the military. During the First World War, the US Army conducted 'morale' surveys to determine how to cheer the troops up enough to make them fight. After the war, the survey designers founded private-sector research organisations. In the following decades, surveys became endemic as HR departments became the 'owners', expanding the question set to satisfaction measures across multiple work areas. As Peter Cappelli and Liat Eldor discuss in the Harvard Business Review[1], this practice ran into some issues in the 1980s when academics figured out that 'satisfaction' was a poor predictor of work performance[2].

Time for a new concept: 'engagement', popularised by psychologist William Kahn in his research into how much 'energy' people brought to their work tasks[3]. Since then, we've been entirely wedded to the annual or twice-yearly employee engagement survey, basing all kinds of interventions on the results, even though many academics remain unconvinced that the results are either valid or valuable. As discussed earlier in the book, global levels of employee engagement on the most popular engagement metrics have remained depressingly low for decades. So, it's clear that something is wrong. Still, the insights from the surveys seem useless at the macro level, given that the picture changes little despite endless interventions in every company administering the surveys.

One major issue with engagement as a concept is that nobody can agree on its meaning. Every HR consultancy has a different definition. Despite this confusion, everybody pretends we agree on what it is and how to measure it. Engagement is now one of the three most-used metrics for setting CEO bonuses and long-term incentive plans[4]. A 2021 CIPD discussion report on employee engagement[5] found that: "Employee engagement is a tricky customer, often seen as contentious and woolly. Numerous definitions and measures exist, and it is often treated inconsistently, being described one moment as a broad umbrella term for an overarching area of people management and the next moment treated as a precise construct that can be convincingly pinned down and measured." The vagueness and confusion have led to some frustrated academics calling for the concept of employee engagement to either be more clearly defined or abandoned altogether[6].

The hand of management consultancies can also be seen in this space, with Gallup's Q12 survey methodology being widely adopted. The 12 questions include ratings of 'role clarity', 'common mission or purpose', and 'strong coworker relationships'. Gallup describes Q12 as assessing "the crucial elements of workplace culture", adding to the confusion by including another disputed term. Some academic researchers have excluded results from Gallup Q12 surveys in their data sets, with one major study[7] citing widespread concerns that the methodology lacked validity. More recently, Gallup's other cash cow product, the CliftonStrengths Assessment (used by over 33m people according to Gallup), has come under fire from academics questioning its reliability and validity[8].

I have two further major issues with engagement surveys. One is a criticism of the methodology. With our innate love of over-simplification, there's invariably a strong focus on the quantitative side of the survey, where answers are averaged to give a single numerical score that you can compare to previous surveys and scores from other organisations. The implicit assumptions of the methodology are:

a. Everybody is answering the same question.
b. They all have the same perspective on the topic.

But this is rarely the case. Let's take an example. A typical survey might ask respondents to rate on a numerical scale how well they feel 'supported' by their immediate manager. The problem with this question is that people have very different interpretations of the meaning of the term 'support' and have diverse support preferences. One employee might view great support as giving them almost total autonomy and briefly checking in occasionally; another might view that as a complete lack of support. Therefore, they are not answering the same question. The survey effectively averages the answers to completely different questions and presents the compounded data as representative – one reason the results should be viewed with some suspicion.

My second criticism is that engagement surveys are essentially infantilising. The philosophy underpinning the process is that the sole responsibility for 'engagement' lies with the employer (the parent), and none lies with the employee (the child). This creates an unhealthy dynamic where employees think the way to solve problems is to complain about them in the survey, with no responsibility on their part to help resolve the issues. Meanwhile, the leaders suck up all the responsibility for trying to solve everything from the top down. It's little wonder that things never seem to get much better.

I once attended a feedback session where the executive team of a bank apologised to employees when *internal communications* received the lowest score on the survey. They outlined plans to add more resources to the internal communications team and increase the frequency of emails. Inevitably, this made little difference to the score in the following survey. A far better conversation might have been to ask the employees what they would do to become more informed. Perhaps asking questions, being curious, interacting with others, seeing what's happening around the business, etc., might be more beneficial than sitting back, complaining and waiting to be spoon-fed information like children. The whole survey and response process feeds the wrong dynamic. Engagement is a two-way process. Yes, employers have a responsibility to engage, but so should employees.

Instead of asking your people the same bland questions as every other company, why not do something useful and original? You probably spend a lot of money segmenting your customers by needs and attitudes, but how much do you really know about your employees? For example, you might find a sizeable segment of working parents. These can typically be found sprinting raggedly every morning from the school dropoff to the train station and doing the same in reverse at the day's end. If you wanted to be inclusive, why not stop scheduling regular meetings before 10 am and after 4 pm? Most meetings are a waste of time anyway. Two birds, one stone?

If you must gather information on how your employees are experiencing the organisation, there may be more valuable ways than the usual survey. In the chapter on transformation programmes, we will meet Dave Snowden, an expert in complexity thinking. Dave has proposed an alternative to the default and intellectually lazy engagement survey. He suggests asking employees to describe their story about the organisation to a relative or neighbour interested in applying for a job there. Dave believes that a combination of sentiment analysis and the richness of the raw narrative could paint a much more nuanced picture of how people perceived their experience working at an organisation. Suppose we understand more about people's perceptions. In that case, it might be easier to shift those rather than endlessly trying to change things that rationally should make a difference (like adding more people to the internal communications team), but seldom do. I think this is worth exploring further.

Nothing should be taken for granted, even if everybody believes it.

— YUVAL NOAH HARARI

13

CAREFUL WHAT YOU WISH FOR: BREAKING DOWN SILOS

I was recently invited to a dinner where one of the topics in a facilitated conversation was: "How do we break down silos to collaborate better?" This is, unfortunately, typical of the poorly framed questions that these types of gatherings explore. There followed much earnest conversation about the attendees' efforts to tackle the lamentable scourge of silos in their businesses.

We have all been conditioned by leadership literature and accepted wisdom to take the simplistic stance that all silos are bad. This is, of course, complete nonsense. No business of any meaningful scale could operate without silos. They are essential to focus, specialisation, and efficiency. They are a beautiful and necessary thing. Silos exist for good reasons: to cluster expertise, streamline work and foster a sense of identity. Much has been written about how silos can lead to turf war, inward focus and lack of collaboration. However, a deeper look will typically uncover the unintended consequences of overly functionally oriented incentives and rewards alongside the predictable effects of power on behaviours.

I suggested as much to my shocked fellow diners. My

example was to consider a large hotel chain business. If I were running such an organisation, I would be very happy to keep my Sales & Marketing team in their silo and my Field Maintenance engineers in theirs. I would want these very different groups to focus on their specialist tasks. They don't need to collaborate. I would not want a busy boiler engineer immersed in the finer technical points of Salesforce Marketing Cloud any more than I would want my head of digital marketing debating the merits of condition-based preventative asset maintenance. They need to focus on where their skills and strengths are.

The key is to exchange relevant information between the two groups at the right time. For example, suppose the Sales & Marketing team sold two weeks of accommodation in one hotel to a group participating in a wheelchair basketball tournament. In that case, the Field Maintenance team should know this and ensure all the elevators are in service and extra maintenance support is on call. Similarly, suppose a hotel's planned exterior maintenance required scaffolding that restricted light to some rooms for a period. In that case, the Sales & Marketing team should be informed to decide whether to take those rooms out of use, discount them, or, at the very least, notify customers in advance to manage expectations.

Yes, there is a case for cross-functional collaboration on specific projects. In the hotel chain example, this might include ensuring a range of views contributed to a project designing the next generation of hotels. However, these types of projects are the exception, not the rule. And they are not without risk. In a Harvard Business Review article titled *Why Employees Who Work Across Silos Get Burned Out*[1], UCL School of Management Professor Martin Kilduff and Associate Professor Sunny Lee summarised their research on the benefits and hidden challenges of focusing on cross-silo collaboration efforts. They looked at the impacts on over 2,000 employees engaged in these efforts (whom they called "boundary spanners"). They found that exposure to strategic information and insights from across the organisation could benefit careers. However, they also found that employees engaged in such collaboration often experienced heightened levels of burnout and were prone to developing negative social behaviours, including abusive behaviour towards colleagues.

So, let's stop the simplistic narrative that 'silos = bad'. Silos are essential. Instead of talking about 'breaking down silos across the organisation' as if that was a) desirable and b) even remotely achievable - why not focus on getting the points of information exchange right?

14

THE DARK SIDE OF EFFICIENCY: DISAPPEARING JOY

With CEOs and senior executives increasingly detached from the worker bees, their logical focus is on efficiency to drive higher profits (helpfully leading to higher bonuses). However, this focus is usually incredibly blinkered, based on a narrow, rational set of easily measured performance indicators. The unintended consequences are the death of joy, the crushing of the human spirit and creativity, and, ironically, the start of unstoppable decline in many cases.

Let's take an experience that is familiar to most of us - the high street coffee shop. On the rare occasion when I go to Starbucks (usually only in motorway services where there's no other choice), I find it a thoroughly depressing experience, utterly devoid of joy and humanity. The décor is identikit, grimy and drab. The employees look depressed. The coffee is grim. The food is unhealthy and processed, likely chosen more for extended shelf life than for nutritional value or taste. Ordering is bizarrely both impersonal and, at the same time, inappropriately personal when they insist on getting your name written on the cup.

I once stayed in a Birmingham hotel with a Starbucks just off the lobby. Running late the following day, I quickly ducked in to grab a coffee on the way to a meeting. When asked for my name, I replied, "I'm the only person here; why do you need my name?" The barista stated that I was required to give her a name as she was obliged by the process to write it on my cup. My reply may have been a little grumpy. Everything in Starbucks has been made bland and miserable by the invisible hand of efficiency. Joy has been entirely killed off. As advertising legend David Ogilvy once said, "Where people aren't having fun, they seldom produce good work."

Things are even worse at Black Sheep Coffee, where the efficiency police have installed those infernal self-ordering screens. Now, instead of a pleasant and human interaction that takes me mere seconds, "Hi, flat white to go, please", I'm forced to navigate multiple screens of choices I don't want while occasionally walloping the screen when it doesn't respond. It's at least ten times more inefficient for me, the bloody customer. I must then join the other poor customers, standing around awkwardly as our orders are prepared and handed over. It's thoroughly dull, with almost no human contact. Ironically, Black Sheep Coffee's tagline is 'Leave the Herd Behind', when all they've done is join the amorphous flock of efficiency joy-killers. More grey sheep than black sheep, I'm afraid.

Contrast this to my two favourite London coffee shops. The first is WatchHouse. They have twenty 'Houses', but no two are the same. The pitch on their website is:

"WatchHouse is a slow take on instant gratification. Thoughtful pours, rare flavour profiles and paraphernalia for your daily cup." Wonderful.

They focus on responsibly sourcing the best quality coffee. The food options are high-quality and beautifully presented, crafted by in-house chefs and bakers. The Houses are exquisitely designed, with contemporary materials and great lighting. Staff are friendly and happy, and I imagine some care has been taken with recruitment, not just a phone call to some miserable temporary staffing agency. Little touches are magical. Your order is delivered to your table. Coffee is served on a wooden tray with a card telling the story of the farmer who produced the coffee beans. And the funny thing is that it's not noticeably more expensive than the miserable, drab and joyless Starbucks version. It's been designed by someone who is not a process and efficiency-driven spreadsheet monkey. Thank God.

My other favourite is Roasting Plant Coffee. Founder Mike Caswell was obsessed with creating the world's freshest coffee. He invented a machine in his garage (called Javabot™) that roasts coffee in micro-batches in every store. But the magical bit is that the machine has a series of translucent vacuum tubes that run across the ceiling from the roaster to the barista machines at the counter. When you order a coffee, the precise amount of the specific beans for your beverage fly magically over your head, drop into the grinder, get instantly ground and used for your super-fresh coffee. It's beautiful, like a Willie Wonka-inspired coffee shop. I love it. I tell everyone who will listen about these two superb businesses. If you have the choice, don't give your money to the dull spreadsheet monkeys at Starbucks, Costa, Nero, or Pret. Instead, invest in joy. The world and your mood will be better for it.

On the subject of customer service, I recently attended an event for a hospitality company's operations teams. The event featured Geoff Ramm, an "inspirational customer service speaker" (according to Geoff) and author of the book *Celebrity Service*. Geoff's speaking style is entertaining, combining stand-up comedy with interesting anecdotes (think Simon Sinek and Billy Connolly had a baby). Geoff did have some genuinely impressive stories about excellent customer service from around the world. In a somewhat predictable outcome, Geoff had tried to codify the "active ingredients" (here we go again) that could, he claimed, be used to train every customer service employee to provide "celebrity" service. Ironically, in Geoff's examples of outstanding service, the magic only happened when employees abandoned their training, ditched all the standard procedures and policies, and did something wholly unscripted and unexpected.

I recently flew to a small airport in France where I was joining a crew for a sailing trip. Lots of safety equipment and supplies resulted in seven checked-in bags - hard to manoeuvre by yourself, even with a trolley. At the car hire desk, I filled in the forms to get my key, and the agent told me there was a long walk to get to the car park. Looking at all my luggage, she told me to go and get a coffee. She closed the counter and ran to the car park to drive my car to the terminal and meet me outside. It was a very kind and helpful intervention that was entirely outside the standard process. I don't think this can be trained. Some people get more joy from helping customers than others. That's why you should ditch the customer service training and the nonsense industry of service standards and manuals and invest more in being careful who you hire to serve your customers.

* * *

Magical and joyful human experiences can happen – but only if you can keep many CFOs, most Private Equity executives, and all process improvement consultants at bay. Efficiency is inevitably only focused on rational and linear perspectives. Notional savings can be made, but at what actual cost? Maybe creating magical experiences costs more on the spreadsheet, but what about happier employees and customers? Could there be a payback in retention, lower absence, better service, and more creativity? Are customers more likely to visit joyful places, spend more and recommend them more frequently? I suspect so. And what about the intangible payback of creating good businesses that add joy and happiness to people's day in a world of ever more predictable, AI-enabled dullness? Surely, that's more satisfying than a short-lived one per cent efficiency gain along the road to mediocrity.

15

A COTTAGE INDUSTRY OF FAILURE: THE GOVERNANCE ILLUSION

To try and ensure that organisations and their leaders behave well, we have created multi-billion-dollar industries of governance and auditing. These industries give us the comforting illusion of assurance, but they merely preserve the status quo. Not only are they spectacularly ineffective at tackling bad behaviour, but they also display a breathtaking deficit of original thought.

If you think for a moment about the board's role, you realise it's rather odd. The board usually plays a significant part in hiring the CEO. Presumably, they make hiring decisions based on their belief that the candidate has integrity and good character. Why then create a system of surveillance and coercion whose implicit assumptions seem to be that the CEO cannot be trusted? Instead, they must be watched over and coerced by financial incentives to make them behave. It's bizarrely parent-child.

The mechanisms of governance include board meetings and committees. Every large corporation appears to have precisely the same governance setup. It's as if they all bought identical governance kits from Governance"R"us. Instant governance -

just add a bunch of worthy former senior executives with a sprinkling of headline diversity but very little original thought. To assure the assurance, as it were, expensive consultants are hired to opine on 'board effectiveness' (whatever that means). These are the same consultants who gave a sound report card to the scores of organisations that later imploded in corporate scandals, but let's not talk about that. PWC's guidance on board assessments[1] includes a list of items on which individual directors should be assessed. In 1st place on the list: *Meeting attendance rate*. In a lowly 6th place: *Understanding of company and industry*.

In my experience of dealing with many boards, I have found that non-executives tend to fall into two camps. The first is the genuinely interested board members who care about the people and the role of the business in broader society. These are relatively rare. The second is the 'portfolio' non-executives, who make a late-stage career out of being on as many boards as they can get away with. Their primary concerns are getting paid more, burnishing their reputation, and ensuring their arses are covered if the shit hits the corporate fan.

On the subject of board remuneration, a report by the Roosevelt Institute[2] noted that "there is strong evidence that companies with higher CEO pay compensate their board members more generously, a clear indication that board members are engaged in a corporate liaison with CEOs rather than serving as independent parties that can assess the appropriate award for a CEO's performance".

When it comes to board governance, the reality is that boards generally have very little idea about what's actually going on in the company. Board reports are carefully constructed with high-level detail by executive teams who are experts in crafting the right messages. Benchmarking is extensively used to hide mediocrity, the message being that it's all OK because we are in line with the competition on these carefully selected metrics. Periodically, the board goes on carefully stage-managed visits to operational sites where they press the flesh and make pleasant small talk with carefully chosen employees for a few minutes before being whisked off to an expensive dinner.

Boards spend significant amounts of time discussing culture, values, incentives, etc. - things that are either meaningless or possibly dangerous. But the uncomfortable truth is that boards rarely learn about unethical behaviour, greed and abuse of power until it's way too late. With hundreds of corporate collapses in the past decade alone and many in scandals, why did the boards fail so miserably in this governance role? Could it be because the whole board construct is outdated, inept, and lazy? How many boards see their role as genuinely challenging the orthodoxy, championing critical thinking, and encouraging the business to think differently from all the others? Not many that I've come across.

* * *

But there is no need to panic because if the board is asleep at the wheel, we have a second line of defence - the annual audit. Recent research by the *Quoted Companies Alliance*[3] showed that audit fees for companies listed on the main London Stock Exchange had rocketed from an average of £730,000 in 2018 to almost £1.3m in 2023, a staggering 78% increase. The Big Four accounting firms (Deloitte, EY, KPMG & PWC) audit 98% of FTSE100 companies and 84% of the FTSE250[4]. Does paying all these exorbitant fees provide a high level of assurance and rigour?

It would appear not. According to research published in 2024 by the *Audit Reform Lab*[5], a think-tank based at Sheffield University, auditors failed to raise the alarm before a staggering 75% of

UK corporate failures. In their report: *Reward for failure: The paradox of audit partners' record payouts amidst poor audit quality,* the researchers examined the audit reports of the largest 250 publicly traded UK companies that collapsed between 2010 and 2022. They concluded that auditors were "failing to perform their core function" and raised "serious concerns that auditors are not challenging enough", noting that 38 of the 250 collapsed companies even declared dividends in their last accounts before imploding. The phrase "fiddling while Rome burns"[*] comes to mind.

The report also notes that from 2020 to 2022, the average pay for Big Four partners rose by 31%. Deloitte partners earned over £1m on average in 2023, with the other Big Four partners close behind. I can't think of any other industry where the rewards for unacceptable failure and incompetence are so perverse.

Despite record fines of over £41m (including investigation costs) issued by the UK's *Financial Reporting Council* in 2023, these equated to less than one per cent of the Big Four's profits[†]. The regulator seems astonishingly toothless. The authors also point out that 75% to 85% of the Big Four's revenues come from non-audit activities, mainly management consulting fees charged to the companies they audit. This raises serious conflict of interest issues and the incentive for the Big Four to prioritise resources for consulting at the expense of auditing.

So, despite all the talk about governance best practices and board effectiveness, we've designed a governance system that's spectacularly useless and obscenely rewarding for the ineffective participants. Fixing the audit circus will probably require legislative action to break up the Big Four, give regulators the

---

[*] The source of this phrase is the story that the Emperor Nero played the fiddle (more probably the lyre) while Rome burned during the great fire of AD 64.
[†] They probably spent more on lunches that year.

power to levy genuinely painful fines, and possibly require auditors to compensate retail investors who lost money due to their incompetence.

Boards, on the other hand, have the freedom to test many different ideas. In our discussion on the effects of power on behaviour and attitudes, we noted that research showed those in powerful positions tended to become detached from those in less powerful positions. They were also more inclined to take risks and condone unethical behaviour. What might some options for mitigation look like?

There may be something to be learned from the German co-determination model, which gives workers legal rights to co-manage corporations. By law, companies with over 2,000 employees must provide 50% of the seats on the Supervisory Board of Directors (equivalent to the Main or Group Board in the UK/US) to workers' representatives. The Supervisory Board elects a Management Board to lead the company. The head of the Supervisory Board is always a shareholder representative who has two votes in case of a deadlock.

It's challenging to identify explicit cause-and-effect outcomes in a complex environment. Still, several studies have suggested that co-determination is one factor that has protected German firms from the worst excesses of corporate greed (notably the far lower prevalence of excessive executive stock options) and short-term thinking. For example, German companies are more likely than their US and UK counterparts to use retained earnings for investment rather than share buybacks.

Having employee representatives on the board may lead to other significant advantages. They bring deep knowledge of how employees and customers are experiencing the organisation, giving the other board members genuine insight they would otherwise not receive. This could help to reduce the detachment effects typically experienced by those in power. Furthermore, executives may be less likely to propose risky or borderline unethical decisions in full sight of those who might be most affected by screwing it up. Finally, employees on the board could help executives understand the reality of the endless organisational nonsense they must navigate to do their jobs. Wouldn't that insight be valuable?

There's no legal requirement to have employees on boards in the US or UK, but there's also no legal impediment. If it seems like a giant leap in one go, why not test the idea by inviting informal employee observers to the board and executive team meetings? And not the usual suspects trotted out - ideally, a random selection to give the best chance of genuinely diverse perspectives. It might be the start of something genuinely worthwhile.

We must no longer accept the lazy, box-ticking, and inept "board effectiveness" assessments. Instead of being congratulated on just turning up and taking the money, what about assessing board directors on different dimensions? These could include:

- Evidence of critical thinking and challenging the status quo or "average" practices passed off as "best".
- Effectiveness in championing evidence-led approaches, particularly in the HR domain.
- Understanding the predictable effects of power and hierarchy and evidence of supporting mitigating strategies for the board and executive teams.
- The insight gained from spending time with customers and employees at varying organisational levels.
- Support for genuine capability building and inclusion, reducing the reliance on consultants and other external parties.

- Doing their research into emerging fads and technologies such as AI, ensuring they are well placed to critically examine the case for any investment and understand the potential risks.
- Ensuring diversity of thinking on the board and executive team and being mindful of the dangers of overly rational, MBA-educated finance professionals becoming the majority faction.
- Testing different approaches to how the board functions - not just meekly following the herd with the same old committees and the same old advisors.

This could be genuinely game-changing if we get it right.

PART III

STUCK IN THE NONSENSE DOOM LOOP: WHY CHANGE IS SO HARD

The brain is a wonderful organ; it starts working the moment you get up in the morning and does not stop until you get into the office.

— ROBERT FROST

16

DEFENCE AGAINST COMMON SENSE: ENDLESS NONSENSE

The Office is not just a TV show; it's a reality for many of us. And while much of this nonsense is farcical and amusing, it's also tragic. It creates self-reinforcing activity loops that consume attention, distract leaders, and effectively defend the organisation against any assault by common sense or new ideas. Sensing that there is little to be gained from calling out the naked emperor, most of us have learned to conform, to go along with the pretence that it all makes sense. The following chapters touch on a few of my favourite manifestations of organisational nonsense, ones you will likely be all too familiar with. After all, they appear to be almost universal.

In workplaces around the world, meetings are where
productivity and creativity go to die.

— ADAM GRANT

17

WHERE DUMB IDEAS MEET FAKE CONSENSUS: THE MEETING

Stephen Rogelberg is a professor of organisational science at the University of North Carolina Charlotte and the author of the bestselling book *The Surprising Science of Meetings*[1]. According to his estimates, there are about 55 million meetings each day in the US, costing somewhere in the region of $1.4 trillion, based on average salary data. In the research for the book, Stephen and his team interviewed 182 senior managers across various industries, finding that 71% said their meetings were unproductive and 65% said that meetings impacted their ability to do actual work. More worryingly, 64% said meetings effectively killed any possibility of deep thinking. If you really want someone in a business to be doing some deep thinking, it's the CEO. Unfortunately, according to a 12-year study[2] by Harvard University's Michael E. Porter and Nitin Nohria, CEOs spend over 70% of their time in meetings and less than 10% with frontline employees and customers. No wonder there's so little original thinking happening. There's no time to think.

COVID-19 lockdowns led to a massive rise in the adoption of virtual meeting technologies, and according to research by the

US National Bureau of Economic Research (NBER), there was a 12.9% increase in the number of meetings per person and a 13.5% increase in the number of attendees per meeting. Quite apart from being a monumental waste of time and mental energy, meetings also encourage the phenomenon of "surface acting", described in the academic literature[3] as "the masking of negative emotions and faking of positive emotions." Studies have noted behaviour such as employees choosing to conceal their fears and frustrations regarding organisational changes discussed in meetings in favour of faking consensus to avoid offending senior leaders proposing the changes[4]. This is how nonsense goes unchallenged. Surface acting during meetings is negatively related to perceptions of both meeting psychological safety and meeting effectiveness[5] and reinforces the effects of the hierarchy of power in the organisation[6].

Far too often, executives consider meetings mere forums for 'cascading' information about planned initiatives and restructures. They neither seek nor expect challenges or honest opinions. Surface-acting ensures that all kinds of half-baked nonsense achieve fake consensus, reinforcing the power distance and the overconfidence of senior leaders.

There are some obvious practical steps to reduce meeting overload, including:

- Fewer, shorter meetings.
- Holding meetings when needed, as opposed to a preset frequency.
- Smaller numbers of attendees.
- Using meetings when decisions are required, not just for sharing information.

Humour and small talk also play a delightfully human role in making meetings more bearable. Surveys among employees who frequently attend workplace meetings suggest that many find them unproductive, a waste of time, and also boring. Lightening the atmosphere through humour and playful activities (such as icebreakers), engaging in small talk before the meeting, and mid-meeting re-energising activities are all associated with higher satisfaction and increased meeting effectiveness[7]. However, the most interesting possibilities lie in ensuring executives and senior managers reframe meetings as opportunities for genuine challenge and debate. Given the power dynamics, this is not an easy task. There are several options to make this process safer for individuals in less powerful roles:

1. Using a *pre-mortem* for proposed initiatives. This is a strategic tool wherein a team imagines an initiative has failed and then works backwards to determine what could lead to the failure. Research suggests[8] that this technique can reduce groupthink and lessen the chances of failure due to heuristics and biases such as overconfidence and planning fallacy[*].

2. *Gamifying* the meeting and for example, using a pre-printed card deck[†] with provocative questions randomly distributed to meeting participants. This potentially removes personal risk. These could include questions like:
   - Is this proposal based on opinions, or do we have any supporting data or research?
   - What would our employees and customers think about this?

---

[*] The planning fallacy is a phenomenon in which predictions about how much time will be needed to complete a future task display an optimism bias and underestimate the time needed.

[†] See www.disruptionspace.co

- What assumptions are implicit in the suggested course of action? Could the opposite be true?
- Is there a way to quickly test this on a small scale before we agree to roll it out?
- How could this make things worse?

Changing the perception of meetings may have some interesting and profound effects. It must be worth some effort.

Forgive me my nonsense, as I also forgive the nonsense
of those that think they talk sense.

— ROBERT FROST

18

CONFUSION IN ACTION: THE DIVERSITY AGENDA

The focus on diversity, equity, and inclusion (DEI) expanded greatly after the shocking murder of George Floyd in 2020 and the subsequent rise of the *Black Lives Matter* movement. Korn Ferry surveyed over 5,000 organisations, 56% of whom said their organisations had established the role of a Chief Diversity Officer post-summer 2020[1]. According to a 2024 report[2], the global DEI market (which includes training, technology platforms, standards, etc.) was valued at USD 10.9 billion in 2023 and is expected to grow to over USD 24 billion by 2030. Almost all large organisations in the US and the UK have implemented DEI initiatives, but there's little evidence yet of meaningful impact.

In a series of highly influential research studies (in 2015, 2018 and again in 2020) that probably did more to put diversity on the executive agenda than anything else, McKinsey claimed their research showed that large public companies with higher racial/ethnic diversity of executives significantly outperformed their less diverse rivals. Quite apart from the usual 'correlation does not prove causation' criticism, when academics revisited the claims for the S&P 500[3], they found no statistically significant differences in any measure of EBIT margin, sales growth, return on assets, return on equity, or total shareholder returns. They concluded that "caution is warranted" in "relying on their findings to support the view that US publicly traded firms can deliver improved financial performance if they increase the racial/ethnic diversity of their executives." I think they were too polite.

Ironically, in some cases, action on DEI initiatives might reinforce the stereotypes the initiatives are trying to overcome. Writing in *Fortune Magazine*[4], researchers Anne Farrell and Michele Frank described their research findings[5] into how an emphasis on diversity shaped managers' beliefs and attitudes when appraising the potential of female subordinates in male-dominated contexts. They found that diversity emphasis sent conflicting signals. On the one hand, the focus on diversity signalled that females were less competent than males and needed more help to succeed. Still, on the other hand, it signalled that females were considered more valuable from a diversity perspective. They concluded that diversity efforts would do little to tackle underlying gender stereotypes and could worsen the situation.

The confusion around DEI terms and aims has also left companies open to accusations of pandering to radical views, particularly on race and gender-related issues. In 2021, Coca-Cola came under fire from conservative critics after an employee leaked pictures of DEI training slides asking white employees to "try to be less white" by being "less ignorant, less arrogant, and less oppressive"[6]. Critics pointed out that the training material was itself highly racist and discriminatory. In the US, conservatives' concerted 'anti-woke' campaign has led to notable employers such as the Ford Motor Company, John Deere, Lowe's and Harley Davidson publicly retreating on sponsoring LGBTQ+ parades and festivals and scaling back other DEI initiatives. The whole DEI space has turned into a politically charged mass of confusion.

Organisations must also be mindful of the unintended consequences of adopting specific quantitative targets for diversity - particularly if these targets are linked to financial incentives. A 2023 enquiry by the UK's Ministry of Defence found that overly ambitious diversity targets for recruitment in the Royal Air Force had resulted in unlawful positive discrimination[7]. The inquiry was triggered by the resignation of a female Group Captain who told senior officers that the policy penalised white men. The investigation found she had faced significant and unreasonable pressure to meet diversity targets. The head of the RAF, Sir Richard Knighton, apologised for the discrimination and a group of 31 men were compensated for being held back in their training due to the targets.

Unconscious Bias Training (UBT) is a staple of DEI everywhere (mainly because it's easy to procure), but there's little evidence that it results in actual behavioural change. Due to budget constraints, the training is often delivered through video-based material in large organisations, turning the whole thing into a giant box-ticking exercise. Research that reviewed the outcomes of diversity training in over 800 large US companies found that the positive effects of mandatory diversity training only lasted a day or two, and there was evidence that it could activate bias or cause a backlash against diversity. As a result, it was linked to either no change or to actual reductions in the number of women in management roles[8].

A review of US corporate diversity training from 1964 to 2008[9] found that employees had to try and internalise what they had heard in cases with no formal follow-up to the training. Many interpreted the learning as having to be careful not to offend minorities. Some felt the message was that all white men were evil. Others assumed that minorities were going to be given their jobs, and a few concluded that minorities just needed to 'toughen up'. In a review of the evidence on unconscious bias and diversity training[10], the UK government's *Behavioural Insights Team* concluded, "The evidence for UBT's ability effectively to change behaviour is limited. Most of the evidence reviewed did not use valid measures of behaviour change."

The intent behind diversity, equity and inclusion is admirable. Discrimination and prejudice have shaped our world for far too long. But in our haste to create efficient and measurable progress, we've overly focused on the easy to measure - gender, race, and sexuality. This has created unintended consequences for the underrepresented groups in focus and missed a critical issue – a severe lack of diversity of thinking. The benefit of having a broader representation in senior leadership roles across these groups is surely diminished if they all went to the same business schools, worked at similar management consultancies or accountancy firms, and exhibited the same rationally focused mindsets. More of the same thinking gives you more of the same results.

So, is there a more accessible and practical way to increase diversity, not just in gender, race, sexuality, etc., but the kind of diversity that ensures lateral thinkers and disruptors get in the door? It turns out that a simple answer might be to batch your hiring or promotions in groups. As Rory Sutherland points out in his book *Alchemy: The Power of Ideas That Don't Make Sense*, research has shown that when hiring people individually, we are more likely to fall back on stereotypes than when we jointly evaluate multiple candidates against each other[11]. Other research suggests that simultaneously selecting multiple candidates (whether for initial hires, promotions or even in elections) leads to more diversity[12]. This instinctively makes sense because you are more likely to take some risk on a quirky candidate in a group hiring situation than in hiring for a single role, where all the eggs are effectively in one basket. Why not take more of an evidence-based approach than follow the diversity herd? The impact might be more meaningful.

19

POINTLESS AT BEST: THE PERFORMANCE APPRAISAL

The annual performance appraisal probably annoys employees more than any other aspect of working life. Most of the other nonsense and noise - internal communications, leaders droning on about values, the annual company report, etc. - can be easily ignored, and doing so presents little career risk. However, the performance appraisal is fraught with emotional risk and, in many cases, financial risk. Despite decades of research showing that individual financial incentives can lead to worse performance and gaming, most organisations cannot resist putting them in place and linking them to the performance appraisal.

Let's deal with financial incentives first. The New York Times bestselling author Dan Pink wrote extensively on this in *Drive: The Surprising Truth About What Motivates Us*[1]. The book's central idea was based on extensive research into human motivation: creating a work environment focused on the things that do motivate us - autonomy, mastery, and purpose – the 'intrinsic motivators', improves employees' performance more than classic 'extrinsic motivators' like financial rewards or the threat of being 'performance managed'. Not only do these extrinsic rewards reliably lead to worse performance, but they've also been shown to reduce collaboration, creativity and self-directed behaviour.

There are many other issues with how financial rewards are constructed. The invention of the 'rewards and incentives design' specialism in HR has made these constructs, particularly at the executive level, ridiculously convoluted and hopelessly open to gaming and other bad behaviour. Despite the rise of so-called experts, there's little evidence that financial incentives increase performance or produce the desired behaviours (invariably and pointlessly linked to corporate values) that many performance management systems pretend to measure.

While leaders in most organisations evangelise about the importance of teamwork and collaboration, those same organisations tend to emphasise individual achievement when it comes to compensation, promotions, rewards, and recognition[2]. Yet a growing body of research indicates that individual incentives might contribute little to team dynamics and may even detract from them[3]. They also fail to recognise other vital dynamics, like the role of 'sacrificers', team members who devote a substantial part of their time to the essential but largely unrecognised work of building better connections within and with other teams. Other research indicates that team-based incentives produce better results, but the conditions under which these can be optimised remain unclear.

At a boutique consulting firm where I worked for several years, Mark, the Managing Director, decided to simplify the rewards for the director team. He wanted to avoid the subjectivity and time-wasting of linking individual rewards to performance appraisals and to limit the risk of individual incentives causing poor behaviour. His answer was to create a profit share where the directors shared a percentage of the company's net profits. Simple to administer, impossible to misunderstand, and pointless to try and game for personal gain. Performance issues were dealt with separately, avoiding conflating the two.

* * *

Things get messy when, as many companies can't seem to resist, you link individual financial incentives to performance appraisals. This becomes an entire cottage industry of nonsense. Performance appraisals, it turns out, are a complete minefield. One of the largest meta-studies of the research was undertaken by Kluger and DeNisi[4]. They reviewed over 3,000 papers and concluded that while receiving performance feedback had a moderate positive effect overall, the picture was wildly variable, with some studies showing no effect at all and over a third showing that performance decreased after appraisal feedback.

A critical factor in the outcome of performance feedback is the extent to which the recipient feels that it is fair and unbiased. Arguably, it can never be impartial, even with the best intentions, as feedback is essentially one person's construct of reality meeting another's. But that aside, let us count the many ways it can go wrong. In a 2016 review[5] of the evidence on performance appraisals, researchers from the *Chartered Institute of Personnel Development (CIPD)* in the UK noted three main categories of rating errors identified by the research. The first is errors where managers' ratings are biased, the second is errors where employees deliberately influence managers' perceptions, and the third is systemic errors due to poorly designed appraisal frameworks and measurement scales. Management rating biases were widespread, and the authors identified over thirteen categories. Some of the highlights were:

- As managers' power increases, they tend to rate

others more negatively and themselves more positively[6].

- When managers receive positive feedback on their performance, they rate their employees higher than if they receive negative feedback[7].
- If a manager hires or recommends an employee, they rate their performance much higher, regardless of actual performance[8].
- If managers like employees, they will give them significantly higher performance ratings than those they dislike, regardless of actual performance[9].

Throw in a bunch of other biases, including gender bias, disability bias, male carer bias, racial bias and others, and then sprinkle manager personality factors on top like agreeableness, conscientiousness, extroversion vs. introversion, etc. (all of which are shown to influence rating scores). In addition, employees try to influence the ratings through ingratiation and self-promotion[10][11]. There's even evidence that employees who constructively challenge the status quo and suggest change tend to receive lower performance ratings[12]. In the end, how can you trust any of it?

The conclusion from the CIPD is that while it would be "unwise to say the least" to suppose that performance appraisals lead to better performance - it would also be "misguided" to suggest they never work and should be scrapped. So that's crystal clear. What a stunningly weak business case for the vast waste of resources, effort and time on a fundamentally biased activity of doubtful value*.

---

* I had no performance appraisals in my three years on the executive team of a FTSE100 organisation. Richard, the CEO, and I would catch up by phone (old school, no video) for 15 minutes every Friday to discuss the week, what was on

A friend who runs a project management consultancy described to me how they abandoned their cumbersome approach to appraisals for something they called the 'Beermat' session. Once every few months, every manager would take direct reports to an individual session, often in a pub. After a good conversation, on one side of a beermat, the employee would note down three areas they were proud of and, on the other side, three areas they wanted to focus on. The beermat would then be kept as a reminder for the next session.

If you must have some type of appraisal, interesting lessons can be learned from the world of self-managing teams. In his book *Reinventing Organizations*[13], author Frederic Laloux describes an alternative peer-based process in which team members evaluate themselves and each other. Each member answers two questions on a scale of 1 to 4:

1. How good have I been at keeping my commitments to the team?
2. How well have I contributed to taking the purpose of the team forward?

They then rated the other team members based on the same two questions. Because they knew others would rate them, individuals tended to be more honest on the self-rating, which generally closely matched the peer rating. When the team's rating was substantially lower than the self-rating, the individual would often realise that things were not going as well as they

---

our minds, and what ideas we wanted to explore. He trusted me to get on with it, which is why he offered me the role in the first place.

thought. They tended to leave independently, avoiding the dreaded 'managing out' experience. Some employees (notably more women than men) rated themselves lower than the team, and this realisation boosted their confidence and self-esteem.

This peer-rating construct might eliminate most of the biases associated with traditional manager-rated performance appraisals. Even if you don't want to move to self-managing teams, why not use the output from a process like this to inform a conversation between managers and their direct reports? Let's leave the last word on this topic to the author Dan Pink, who sensibly suggests that the best thing to do is to hire good people and just leave them alone.

I have a private plane. But I fly commercial when I go
to environmental conferences.

— ARNOLD SCHWARZENEGGER

20

GREENWASHING AND HOT AIR: THE "E" IN ESG

The Paris Agreement is a legally binding international treaty on climate change. It was adopted at the 2015 UN Climate Change Conference (COP21). The agreement's overarching goal is to "hold the increase in the global average temperature to well below two °C above pre-industrial levels" and pursue efforts "to limit the temperature increase to 1.5°C above pre-industrial levels".

The signing of the agreement sparked shareholder pressure as large organisations were scrutinised for their role in protecting the environment. Most settled on the 'Net Zero' concept - a notional balance of carbon emissions and sinks. In 2016, many CEOs and executive teams, having no clue how to achieve net zero, pushed the deadline out to 2030 or beyond, secure in the knowledge that they would be long gone before the organisation was measured on any of these vague commitments. Happy days. Box ticked. Even worse, many saw an opportunity for dishonest virtue signalling to try and appear more responsible to employees and customers. Why does this matter? Because many consumers try to make ethical choices regarding their spending. The market for ethical spending in the UK was valued at £122bn in the UK in 2023[1]. Greenpeace defines 'green-washing' as: "a PR tactic used to make a company or product appear environmentally friendly, without meaningfully reducing its environmental impact."

McDonalds is one of the largest beef buyers in the world, and by some estimates, it uses over two billion pounds of beef every year. Livestock farming uses vast resources and is estimated to account for almost 15% of global greenhouse gas emissions[2]. In a brilliant example of greenwashing, McDonald's announced in 2019 that it was introducing paper straws (don't look over there; look over here), which turned out to be almost impossible to recycle.

Innocent Drinks in the UK sells fruit-based drinks in single-use plastic bottles. It's owned by the Coca-Cola company, the world's leading plastic polluter, according to the 2023 Brand Audit[3] by *Break Free From Plastic*. In 2022, Innocent launched a TV advertising campaign featuring cuddly animated characters encouraging consumers to "get fixing up the planet" by buying Innocent products. The UK's Advertising Standards Authority swiftly banned the advertisements. It ruled that the ads implied that buying Innocent drinks "was a choice which would have a positive environmental impact when that was not the case".

Keurig Dr Pepper recently paid a $1.5m civil penalty and agreed to comply with a 'cease and desist' order after the US Securities and Exchange Commission (SEC) accused the firm of making misleading statements about the recyclability of its single-use coffee pods.

In 2021, the *Changing Markets Foundation* looked at a range of clothing from major high-street fashion brands to check the truthfulness of their sustainability claims. A shocking 60% overall were found to be misleading, with H&M leading the pack at 96% misleading in their view[4].

Unilever, the global FMCG brand, was the world's third

leading plastic polluter in the 2023 Brand Audit. But you could easily be fooled by their famous logo, designed by the Wolf Olins agency, featuring motifs of bees, birds and plants inside a large U shape. It looks like a logo for organic baby shampoo. In 2020, Unilever's LinkedIn campaign celebrated the company's 90th year of operations with the hashtag *#90yearsofdoinggood*. Unilever's employees appear to live in a parallel reality, where they think they are sustainable superheroes even as the company's plastic fills up the world's oceans. It's taken them decades to figure out that you can sell laundry detergent capsules in a cardboard box instead of a plastic one, yet they haven't even completely phased out the plastic ones. It seems completely ridiculous.

It's hugely disingenuous to tout your plastic products as recyclable when you know that globally, over 90% of them will never be recycled. The situation is even worse in the US, where the plastic recycling rate was estimated to have declined to about 5–6% in 2021, down from a high of 9.5% in 2014 and 8.7% in 2018 when the U.S. exported millions of tons of plastic waste to China and counted it as recycled even though much of it was burned or dumped[5].

Many large organisations, such as Microsoft and BP, base some of their net-zero strategies on purchasing 'carbon credits', primarily based on planting trees in places like California. In an ironic turn of events, recent catastrophic forest fires, blamed on a failure to tackle climate change, have wiped out many trees that were supposed to provide the carbon offset buffer, leaving the whole scheme under question.

According to UN forecasts, plastic waste is set to triple by 2060, global meat consumption is trending upward, and deforestation continues at pace. Fashion retailers are accelerating their production of garments using fossil-fuel-based fabrics. Global temperatures keep breaking records. While most large companies make no meaningful efforts to change, they invest more in PR and spin than practical and impactful activity.

There's increasing evidence of tactics such as blame-shifting, denial, and doubt, which proved so effective for tobacco companies for decades to avoid litigation and penalties. These were memorably described in the 2010 book *Merchants of Doubt*[6]. ExxonMobil had, until 2004, regularly paid for advertorials in the New York Times that questioned whether climate change is real or whether it is caused by humans, even though internal documents indicate that the company had little doubt on the matter[7].

Large-scale polluters like BP often adopt science-related imagery and green-sounding slogans (e.g."We care about generations to come"). BP even rebranded to *"Beyond Petroleum"*. In a strategic update in February 2022[8], BP announced that it expected to "increase the proportion of its capital expenditure in transition growth businesses to more than 40% by 2025 and is aiming for around 50% by 2030". Only a year later, the company announced that it was slowing its planned oil and gas output cuts from 40% to 25% by 2030 (compared with 2019 levels). In November 2024, BP announced it would halt all new offshore wind projects and scrap eighteen early-stage hydrogen projects. Perhaps a further rebrand to *"Back to Petroleum"* would be more honest.

I'm not generally a fan of the 'big state,' but this requires coordinated government action. Corporations like BP, Unilever, and the Coca-Cola Company will never 'do the right thing' by themselves, even if it's one of their corporate values...eyeroll.

There's also growing evidence that emerging independent certifications and 'eco-labels' promising to safeguard against greenwashing are themselves open to gaming and greenwashing. LEED (Leadership in Energy and Environmental Design) is the world's most widely used green building rating system. A

2020 study[9] examining the certification process illustrated that firms can accrue points without actually reducing emissions, which is the program's goal. Another study of UK-based B Corps* found that certified firms underperformed or failed to contribute to environmental reduction goals[10].

2030 is not far away, so many organisations will need to revisit their commitments and implement shorter-term targets to assess progress and be honest about the challenges that faster progress might pose to the profitability of their business models. Ironically, without more transparency, shifting government policies towards incentivising progress through grants or tax breaks will be more challenging.

---

* From the B-Lab UK website: Certified B Corporations, or B Corps, are companies verified by B Lab to meet high standards of social and environmental performance, transparency and accountability.

21

DANGEROUS ARTEFACTS: THE ORGANISATION CHART & OTHER VOODOO

The first iteration of the now ubiquitous organisation chart appeared in the New York & Erie Railroad records around 1854. Unlike modern organisation charts, which remind us who's in charge by having the CEO at the top and the workers at the bottom, this chart was a creative attempt to show how the railroad company worked in practice and how information flowed into the different branches of the railway lines. Nowadays, almost all organisation charts are the same: bland, top-down representations of a simplified world and its imaginary lines of control. I can't think of any other example in modern life where so many decisions are made using a model that is so unrepresentative of the real world.

Early in my career, I came across a graphic on the internet entitled *The Real Organization Chart*. It had the usual boxes and lines, but the boxes had smiley and frowny faces instead of job titles or names. But the most hilarious thing about the picture was that the chart was covered with arrows indicating what was really happening. The captions on the arrows included *secret crush, sells drugs to, hates, knows about corruption, religious connection, secret deal, supports the same football team, kids in the same*

*school, plays golf with, having an affair, runs office lottery (unfairly),
owes favours to* and many others. Brilliant. The contrast between
this and the standard organisation chart was sublime. Humour
only made it more obvious.

What on earth makes us think that organisational charts are
helpful in making decisions about the future of our organisations? They entirely ignore the fundamentally complex (but
fascinating) nature of human systems. The fallacy of the organisation operating in a way that resembles the organisational
chart probably explains the sense (from both employees and
customers) that getting the simplest things done in large organisations seems to be incredibly difficult.

It also may go some way towards explaining why the ways of
working never entirely change as expected after restructuring
efforts. Moving the little boxes around on the chart doesn't often
seem to lead to the expected performance outcomes of restructuring. Researchers who examined the result of restructuring
across a range of small firms, large European companies, and
U.S. Fortune 50 firms[1] found that restructuring decreased profits
by 2.6% on average (a $57m hit for the largest firm in the study).
Other research literature reviews[2] have concluded that there is
strong evidence that restructuring can devastate employee
morale, lead to loss of loyalty and trust in the organisation and
generate feelings of insecurity and confusion.

But for me, there are two other cardinal sins of organisation
charts. The first is that they dehumanise the organisation
entirely. Senior executives considering 'downsizing' or 'rightsizing' the structure can stay detached from the human consequences of their decisions to delete or reduce the size of a few
boxes, decisions that may affect the lives of hundreds of others.
This must only reinforce the sense of detachment caused by
high power levels. Secondly, individuals with natural talent and
potential are invariably hidden in the anonymous team-sized

boxes at the bottom of the hierarchy. They will never be discovered because they are invisible there.

In early 2021, I needed to assemble a small team to help conduct a strategic review of a large real estate business I was working for. I decided to experiment with an internal advertisement which said: "Wanted: individuals for a 6-month secondment to a new strategy team. Applications are welcome from colleagues in any role or any location. You must be curious. Please apply creatively." No other guidance was given. I received 35 applications. Pin, a Malaysian national who had come to the UK as an international student, was a team leader in one of the company's 150 buildings. In his application process, he convinced the CEOs of several companies he admired to let him interview them. He then presented his findings on their strategies and innovation tactics. I hired him immediately. James, an area manager, sent me a video of him jogging around south London, interspersed with snippets about different work projects and interests outside work. At the end of the video, he zoomed in on his Strava app to reveal that the course he ran across London spelt out 'Hire Me' in giant letters on the map. Hired. With Vicki and Ericka's additions, I found four incredibly talented individuals who brought a completely different perspective on customers (some of whom interacted with them daily), how the business functioned, and all the nonsense they had to surmount to give the customers good service. They also brought an impressive informal network that operated entirely outside the formal hierarchy of the organisation chart.

A month before the business was due to launch an expensive marketing campaign, I saw that the Trustpilot rating was 1 star (the lowest rating possible; there's no zero). I guessed that only unhappy customers were giving feedback, which didn't reflect the broader customer experience. I inquired why nothing was being done about this and was told that nobody in the organisation had 'been made accountable' for it. I pulled the team together and challenged them to get us to 4-star in four weeks. Unfazed, they activated their informal network, where they had longstanding friendships in many operational parts of the business. This broader group got going immediately by speaking to customers face-to-face and asking them to rate the company on Trustpilot. Three weeks and 12,000 reviews later, the rating hit four stars. This only worked because it completely bypassed the command and control structures of the organisation chart and gave the team full autonomy to take on the challenge.

Job descriptions are equally useless, with most comprising a lengthy list of the blindingly obvious process elements of the job. It's amusing that many organisations talk about agility when all their job descriptions are rigid and uninspiring. Worse still, job descriptions often say silly things like "full accountability for the marketing function" as you move into more senior roles. This sets the perfect conditions for defending 'turf' and the excuse for not allowing anyone else to challenge the thinking or activities in that functional area. It's a recipe for mediocrity. Outside of the creative industries, you'll struggle to find a job description that mentions critical thinking, creativity, experimentation, generating new ideas, welcoming constructive conflict and challenge, or looking outside the sector for inspiration—all the things that could make a real difference to the organisation and make work far more fulfilling for the employees.

There's real hidden talent everywhere. Why don't we get out of the way and let it emerge? Some of the ways might include:

- Creating project or secondment opportunities without preconceived notions about the required experience, qualifications or seniority.
- Setting up "hackathons" focused on specific business problems where any employee can come and explore their ideas on solving the issues.
- Creating ways to crowdsource ideas from across the organisation, involving employees who submitted the best ideas in the implementation.

You will be surprised at how much talent is hidden in your organisation. It just needs a little effort and some thinking differently to uncover it.

22

STUPIDITY AT SCALE: THE TRANSFORMATION PROGRAMME

The transformation programme can potentially be the pinnacle of stupidity at work. It offers the opportunity to combine a broad array of misguided beliefs to ensure the stupidity of the whole is even more significant than the sum of its parts. The transformation programme is often:

- Instigated by an overconfident CEO or executive, sure of their ability to predict and control the future.
- Planned in stages with 'deliverables' and 'outcomes' pre-defined.
- Based on an oversimplified model of how the organisation functions.
- Influenced by the latest management fads created by management consultants and leadership gurus.
- Designed by the same consultants using context-free methodologies that assume the future will oblige in changing to match their PowerPoint slides.
- Set up to consider any dissenting views as 'resistance to change' that must be 'change managed' rather than thoughtfully considered.

- Driven by an entirely rational logic, completely ignoring humans' irrational and emotional nature.
- Based on a business case focused on a narrow perspective of efficiency gains, which limits the potential for creativity and joy.

In 2021, Oxford University's Said Business School and EY formed a research collaboration[1] to study where transformation programmes go wrong and how best to respond when they do. Of the executives involved in the study, 67% reported experiencing at least one underperforming transformation effort in the preceding five years. That represents an enormous waste of time, money, and emotional energy.

According to their research, 96% of transformation programmes experienced a 'turning point' when they deviated from their course. Leadership was forced to intervene, often unsuccessfully. The 96% essentially represents an endemic over-confidence bias. The Said / EY report criticises the overly rational approach to transformation based on outdated views and models and a preoccupation with linear logic and causality - the 'if I do x, I will get y' fallacy. Unfortunately, for those with a rational and linear disposition, things never quite pan out like that.

Interestingly, the recommendations include a) remembering that transformations at their heart are about people and all their human experiences and emotions; b) not trying to slavishly stick to the original transformation plan as new information emerges; and c) navigating the 'turning points' through an iterative process the authors described as *Sensing, Sense-making,* and *Acting*. The authors go on to say:

"If our research over the past three years has made one thing clear, it is that organisations need to treat transformations as dynamic and continual learning processes characterised by periods of shifting emotional energy. These dynamics are not to be managed back into the original plan."

This research is genuinely interesting and thoughtful. For a contrasting 'old school' simplistic rational viewpoint, try this from consultancy Oliver Wyman. In their view,[2] there are "two types of causes for business transformation struggles", the first being "structural deficiencies, such as the lack of a unified vision and roadmap with clear milestones that teams are held accountable to, or the absence of risk management process", and the second are "cultural pitfalls" where "transformation calls for different ways of working, including a level of cross-organisational collaboration that might feel unnatural for many organisations that are used to operating in silos." So, it seems the answer, in their view, is simple: more rational thinking, more process and addressing the pitfalls of something imaginary. Good luck with that approach. Do write to me if it works.

* * *

The findings and the recommendations from the Said / EY report are remarkably consistent with insights from complexity science, the study of complex adaptive systems. In complexity science, a 'complex system' comprises many interacting components. Examples include the human immune system, the Earth's global climate, and social systems like cities and large organisations.

The behaviour of a complex system is intrinsically challenging to model because of the many dependencies, relationships, and other types of interactions between its components and the system itself, as well as between the system and its external environment. Complex systems have distinct properties that arise from these relationships, such as nonlinearity[*], emergence[†], spontaneous order[‡], and adaptation[§].

Dave Snowden[3] is a Welsh management consultant and researcher in the application of complexity science in organisations. Dave is particularly well known for developing the Cynefin Framework while working at IBM, describing the framework as a 'sense-making device'[4]. The framework suggests four primary decision-making contexts or 'domains': *Clear, Complicated, Complex,* and *Chaotic.* Snowden asserts that to make good decisions, you must first understand which domain you are operating in.

In the *Chaotic* domain, cause and effect are untethered. The only valid way to respond is by taking immediate action, any action, to try to regain order. Examples in this realm include terrorist attacks, market meltdowns, natural disasters, etc. The leader's job here is first to act, then sense where stability is present and missing, then respond (approach: *Act, Sense, Respond*). In so doing, the hope is to transform the situation from chaotic to complex - where identifying emerging patterns can help prevent future crises, and new opportunities may arise.

The *Clear* domain is the realm of 'known knowns', where cause-effect is apparent in that doing 'x' reliably gives you 'y'.

---

[*] In mathematics and science, a nonlinear system is one in which a change of output is not proportional to the change of the input. More X might not give you more Y.

[†] In philosophy, systems theory, science, and art, emergence occurs when a complex system has properties or behaviours that its parts do not have on their own and emerge only when they interact in a wider whole.

[‡] Typically used to describe the emergence of various kinds of social orders from the behaviour of a combination of self-interested individuals who are not intentionally trying to create order through planning. E.g., how people in a neighbourhood self-organise after a natural disaster strikes.

[§] The behaviour of the system may not be predictable according to the behaviour of its components. It is adaptive in that the individual and collective behaviour mutate and self-organise in response to a change-initiating event.

The advice here is to establish the facts, categorise the problem, and respond by applying best practice (the approach is: *Sense, Categorise, Respond*). Snowden cautions that this approach only works for highly straightforward issues.

The *Complicated* domain is the land of the 'known unknowns'. There is a relationship between cause and effect, but it requires analysis or expertise to uncover. There's a range of answers to solve the problem. Good practice exists, but there is no single 'best practice'. Here, the advice is to assess the facts, analyse, and apply good practice (approach: *Sense, Analyse, Respond*). Designing a bridge might be a good example. This is the world of engineers, lawyers and experts. Artificial intelligence copes well here due to rationality. However, this approach is highly unlikely to work in the *Complex* domain. The observant reader may note this is essentially the logic behind the Harvard Case Study Method we discussed earlier.

By contrast, the *Complex* domain is the world of 'unknown unknowns'. This is the domain of organisational change and transformation. Cause-effect can often only be deduced in retrospect when you look back at what happened. It's extremely difficult to predict the outcomes of any intervention. There is no 'best' or even 'good' practice; there is only 'emergent' practice from experimenting and learning. The advice here is to probe the system with multiple small interventions, see what patterns emerge, and amplify the helpful patterns while dialling down the unhelpful (approach: *Probe, Sense, Respond*). In the *Complex* realm, experts are dangerous. They bring preconceived solutions as baggage. They are likely to assume the issue is only complicated when it's complex and to attempt to apply good practices from other contexts. Deploying management consultants with an allegedly 'proven approach' to transformation will likely be a recipe for disaster here.

As highlighted in the Said / EY report, transformation efforts often fall into this trap. Although the recommendations in the report on how to approach the 'turning points' use a slightly different language (*Sense, Sense-make, Act*), the sentiment is strikingly similar to the *Complex* domain approach advocated by Snowden. Both call for a more nuanced, humble, and collaborative approach. They both advocate for exploring emerging signals and patterns. Both talk about 'sensing' before acting and the emergent and iterative process. They both advise taking smaller steps by testing multiple small interventions to learn.

In the concluding remarks of the Said / EY report, the authors call for "a new archetype of leadership that counters some of the outdated authoritarian beliefs we have inherited from the 20th century." I am all for that. This should include abandoning the nonsense of *change management*; a pseudo-discipline focused on finding frameworks to reliably apply in any context to try to "manage" the outcomes so they match the PowerPoint plan. It's a complete waste of time and energy.

The report's authors conclude that our ability to experience, feel, and emotionally respond differentiates us from AI. They say that "within those emotional responses are deep learnings and potential for huge accelerations in progress." I couldn't agree more. This is the human potential at risk from AI unless we get our act together - more on this next.

PART IV

EFFICIENCY OR HUMANITY?
AI & THE TURING TRAP

The danger of AI is not that it will become too intelligent, but that we will become too stupid.

— YUVAL NOAH HARARI

23

A QUICK PRIMER: WHAT IS GENERATIVE AI?

Artificial Intelligence is already embedded in many aspects of our day-to-day life. Every time you use your credit card, log on to Netflix or search the internet, AI algorithms work in the background to verify your identity, predict the kind of shows you would like, or show you personalised search results. Many of these algorithms were costly to build and took years of effort to make reliable, relying on armies of coders.

The new frontier of this technology is Generative AI, which is based on powerful computer models known as large language models (LLMs). These models are repeatedly trained to predict the next word in a sentence. As they assimilate hundreds of billions of words, they become increasingly adept at understanding the outputs to predict different contexts. OpenAI's ChatGPT is the best-known model, but many others are in development.

Examples of tasks that LLMs can carry out include writing, reading, and chatting. More recently, the capabilities have expanded to include generating images, audio and video.

Although the technology is extremely powerful, the models currently have several limitations. These include:

- *Knowledge cutoffs* - the models know nothing past the last date of the data set they were trained on (October 2023 in the case of the free-to-use version of ChatGPT as of October 2024).
- *Bias & toxicity* - as the models were trained with broad access to information on the internet, they were exposed to prejudice and toxicity in the training material. In a highly embarrassing 2016 example, Microsoft had to turn off 'Tay', its AI chatbot, after Twitter users tricked it into posting a series of racist tweets, including: "Hitler was right, I hate the Jews". Recently, AI companies have been making progress in reducing bias and increasing safety.
- *Hallucinations* - AI occasionally makes things up, confidently presenting 'hallucinations' as facts. In 2023, a New York lawyer was sanctioned[1] after submitting a legal brief in a federal case that relied on fake judicial opinions in fictional legal cases made up by ChatGPT.
- *Input & output limitations* - most models can accept a limited size of prompt and have limits on the size of the output.
- *Difficulty handling structured data* - the models are better suited to unstructured data (e.g., text, images, etc.) than structured data (e.g., the type of tabular data typically found in spreadsheets).

Regarding how AI is used in a work context, Andrew Ng, the former head of the Google Brain team, suggests that thinking about two distinct constructs is helpful. The first is *Web interface-*

based LLM applications, where users enter prompts into a web-based interface to receive the outputs. An example might be a busy employee using AI to help summarise a document before a meeting to discuss the document's conclusions. The second is *Software-based LLM applications*, where the AI technology is embedded into other systems in the workplace and needs context-specific information about your organisation. An example might be an AI chatbot that instigated a customer returns process for an online retailer.

Very specialist AI models have captured the public attention by surpassing human capabilities in tasks such as image recognition, with applications such as self-driving vehicles and accurate medical diagnosis from Magnetic Resonance Imaging (MRI) scans. However, in some ways, the general-purpose nature of AI is what makes it such a disruptive technology. It's potentially applicable to any workplace tasks that involve reading, writing, or verbal interactions - making the possibilities almost endless. But so are the potential consequences, which require careful and holistic consideration of impacts and ethics both at organisational and societal levels.

The big management consultancies are hyping AI for all they are worth, predicting considerable changes in the workplace by 2030 (although, as we saw earlier in our discussion on consultant-generated fads, most of their predictions turn out to be hopelessly inaccurate). McKinsey's May 2024 report, *A new future of work: The race to deploy AI and raise skills in Europe and beyond*,[2] suggests that up to 30% of current work hours could be automated by 2030, leading to 12 million "occupational transitions" (presumably a more politically correct term for job losses).

Herein lie the risks of thoughtlessly jumping on the latest fads and the frantic sense of urgency manufactured by management consultants. The message being pushed out is: "If you're not an early adopter, you're already too late". There's an enormously high risk of doing idiotic things, calling to mind a quote attributed to author Robert Charles Wilson: "Stupid people do stupid things, but people who are smart enough can do something really stupid."

The factory of the future will have only two employees, a man and a dog. The man will be there to feed the dog. The dog will be there to keep the man from touching the equipment.

— WARREN BENNIS

24

THE TURING TRAP: WHY CEOS
NEED TO TREAD CAREFULLY

I n May 2023, a very curious thing happened. A group of the most influential thinkers and leaders in the AI industry (including the CEOs of OpenAI and Google DeepMind) signed an open letter[1] warning that the technology they were building might one day pose an existential threat to the human race. These fears appear to be based on three factors:

1. In their race to create ever more capable machines that seek to replicate human intelligence, technologists are releasing technologies they are not entirely in control of. For example, how many AI models actually learn is unclear to their creators. They have become 'black boxes' that continue to be unpredictable.
2. CEOs and business executives, in cahoots with management consultancies, may go too far in the quest to replace humans in the name of efficiency and might inadvertently hand over too much control to AI, with unknown consequences.

3. Governments and policymakers will not understand the rapidly changing landscape and its ethical and societal implications in time to assert any control over the outcomes.

These three concerns are similar to those identified in the influential paper *The Turing Trap: The Promise & Peril of Human-Like Artificial Intelligence*[2], written by Erik Brynjolfsson, Director of the Stanford Digital Economy Lab. In it, the author argues that the societal impact of AI will depend on whether its primary use is to augment human jobs or automate them. He makes the compelling argument that when AI augments human capabilities, the space of possibility for innovation and value creation is far more significant than the space of mere automation.

When the focus is on replicating and automating jobs currently done by humans, opportunities for new value creation are stifled, and people are no longer required. This would inevitably result in even higher inequality than we already have, creating an 'underclass' of effectively unemployable people trapped in a system where they have no realistic prospect of breaking out. The implications go beyond immediate employees, affecting families, communities, and society. As a warning from the past, the author points to declining life expectancy, increasing suicides and an epidemic of opioid usage in parts of the US where unemployment is rife, particularly in areas that were once manufacturing heartlands.

CEOs and executives will inevitably be drawn to the lure of automation as this appears to be more accessible and promises more notional gains in the short term (even though automating a whole job turns out to be incredibly difficult in practice). If you just swap people for machines, you don't have to make radical changes or innovate. On paper, it's the quickest route to efficiency and the easiest way to provide evidence to analysts and shareholders that you are embracing AI at pace and moving to a scalable model (i.e., growth without more people). It also eliminates all the difficulties of hiring, retaining, and engaging people and dealing with the demands of working from home, burnout, and mental health.

Even better, because governments and policymakers can't see what might be coming, there are no incentives to favour augmentation over automation. It's the very opposite. There's a good chance that developing an AI project might attract R&D tax credits. Project costs of deploying AI can probably be treated as capital expenditure. Fewer people on the payroll means less tax paid to the government. Happy days!

And so, the stage is set for really stupid things to be done. As I write this, the forces of stupidity are massing on the borders of organisations everywhere. As a matter of some urgency, CEOs and executive teams need to:

1. Resist the automation-focused overtures of management consultants and pause to explore the full range of possibilities and potential consequences of AI. This doesn't require you to be a technologist! If this question does not squarely fit in the "Social" and "Governance" of your Environmental, Social & Governance (ESG) policy, I'm not sure what does.
2. Understand that overly focusing on automation and efficiency will severely limit the opportunities for genuine transformation and innovation, and there will be a high chance of disappointment.
3. Have the courage and ambition to consider AI as a catalyst for the broader transformation of the business, taking a stand on genuinely putting humanity first. (More on this in Part IV).

In tandem, governments and policymakers must start considering how to remove perverse incentives that encourage and reward automation and replace them with incentives to promote augmentation and innovation. This could be relatively straightforward, with tax breaks or grants on AI augmentation linked to maintained employment, new product development, shared gains, etc. However, it is now urgent as things are moving rapidly, and the risks of shortsighted business decisions that aggregate to poor societal consequences are extraordinarily high.

25

EFFICIENCY: WHY EVERYBODY
IS WORSE OFF SOMETIMES

Making decisions based on rational notions of efficiency is fraught with danger but all too common. Sometimes, efficiency makes everybody worse off. LinkedIn has been an early and enthusiastic adopter of AI. The premium subscription includes access to an AI-powered job assessment tool. The tool uses AI to quickly advise you on the best way to tweak your CV for any role. Once that's done, you can apply for any job with a single click. If a cover letter is mandated, a quick prompt to ChatGPT with a cut-and-paste of the job blurb will produce it in seconds. In my estimation, the effort to apply for a job has been reduced by a factor of 90% or more.

What a great poster child for AI and automation. Or is it? Previously, only people genuinely interested in a role would take the time and effort to apply. There was at least some disincentive for speculative applications. Now, people fire off applications many times a day just in case one might land. It's 'ready, fire, aim'. It's not unusual to see over 1,000 applicants per advertised role on the platform now.

Although recruiters also have AI to filter the applications, the task is almost impossible because, by at least some anecdotal accounts, up to 90% of the applications have been optimised by the same AI. So, how can you tell them apart? There's no way for the best applicants to stand out. This results in a highly odd situation where the role remains unfilled despite thousands of applicants. Most applicants don't even get the courtesy of a response. Efficiency and automation have made things immeasurably worse for both parties.

When we automate jobs, we invariably only look through a rational lens at the obvious. I once spent a fascinating few weeks observing the behaviours and strange dynamics of the Milton Keynes railway station passenger services team. They were often nowhere to be found when passengers needed help or information - particularly the spectacularly inept station management team who made hiding from passengers their primary activity. The most helpful person in the station was a cleaner who worked for an agency. She regularly interrupted her sweeping and mopping to help passengers get information or navigate the almost impossible task of buying a train ticket using the world's worst-designed ticket machines. She kept an eye on criminal activity and even alerted the station staff if she thought that people could be a danger to themselves (suicide being a significant issue on the railway). I later found out that she had been replaced with a robot cleaner. That's a tragedy for all.

The risks associated with overly rational efficiency increase exponentially when the jobs we try to replace with AI have highly emotional nuances. Let's take an example. Primary school classrooms in the UK are staffed by a Teacher and a Teacher Assistant. Right now, I know the Teacher Assistant role is being targeted, with suggestions that substantial efficiency savings are available if some are replaced with AI versions.

On a spreadsheet, this makes perfectly rational sense. The job description includes tasks such as prepping lesson plans, answering questions about classroom tasks, marking homework, and assisting with parents' queries. AI-powered assistants could be trained to perform many of these tasks. Given the financial difficulties of most state-run schools, the cost savings could be significant and attractive. This represents the classic efficiency-driven rational business case.

The problem is that the job description comes nowhere close to describing the complexity of what Teacher Assistants do. I know this because I have close friends who do this job, which is incredibly undervalued. They have many stories to tell. In addition to their more apparent tasks, they fulfil unsung but vital roles. Teacher Assistants watch out for children who come from neglected homes. They often spend their own money buying neglected children breakfast so they have the energy to learn. They sometimes provide underwear and clean clothing and even quietly treat them for head lice, worms, or other parasites. The genuine love and care these kids get from Teacher Assistants is often their only stability in a world of chaos and neglect. Their futures might depend on it. Teacher Assistants also develop deep bonds with children who have special educational needs, encouraging them and creating a safe environment for them to make real progress. I've heard stories of parents who broke down in tears of gratitude when their child, who had never spoken before, was helped to speak for the first time. In another important aspect of the role, Teacher Assistants act as emotional and sometimes even physical support for their teachers, who must deal with the dark side of education when they face abuse or assault by pupils or even parents.

AI can't do any of these things, but they are all essential.

Herein lies the danger of rational thinking in a complex and emotional world. We must never rely on organisation charts, paper job descriptions, dry process maps, or other overly rational paraphernalia to guide our decisions about using AI to replace people. There will be unanticipated human costs that might vastly outweigh the notional efficiency savings. However, if approached correctly, we might unlock tremendous potential in the complementarities between humans and technology.

So long as we are conscious of avoiding the Turing Trap and the dark side of rational thinking, we should seek to explore the exciting transformative promise of AI and other emerging technologies. Genuinely augmenting human capabilities could be a game-changer.

26

THE CON OF EARLY ADOPTION: CAUTIONARY TALES

For a year or two now, the rhetoric from the big consulting firms is that if you've not already adopted AI, you'll be too late to the game, and your competitors will have an unassailable lead. Luckily, that's rubbish. If anything, competitors will have wasted a ton of cash and resources, annoyed their employees and customers in vain, and sometimes had to unwind it all when AI was a disaster. These examples should serve as cautionary tales.

Zillow's machine-learning algorithm costs the business USD 540 million, leading to 2,000 job losses.

In February 2021, Zillow, a leading US real estate marketplace, announced that it would leverage its AI-generated home valuation tool to make cash offers to home sellers seeking a quick sale[1]. In a press release, Zillow's Chief Operating Officer Jeremy Wacksman said: "This is a proud moment for Zillow's tech team and speaks to the advancements they've made in machine learning and AI technology." Nine months later, Zillow announced that it was exiting its Zillow Offers business[2], closing the division with a loss of 2,000 jobs and writing off $540 million after overpaying for houses they were forced to sell at a loss. The algorithm was baffled by unusual movements in the US housing market post-Covid. "We've determined the unpredictability in forecasting home prices far exceeds what we anticipated, and continuing to scale Zillow Offers would result in too much earnings and balance-sheet volatility," said Rich Barton, Zillow's co-founder and CEO (somewhat red-faced, I imagine).

NYC's Microsoft-powered chatbot advises small businesses to break the law.

In October 2023, New York City Mayor Eric Adams announced that an AI-powered chatbot developed with Microsoft would help New York business owners navigate government regulations. In March 2024, The Markup[3] (a "nonprofit newsroom that investigates how powerful institutions are using technology to change our society") reported that the AI chatbot was telling businesses to break the law[4]. Ironically, the chatbot was launched shortly after the Mayor's fanfare announcing the release of a comprehensive *New York City Artificial Intelligence Plan*[5]. This plan, the Mayor said, would "empower city agencies to deploy technologies that can improve lives while protecting against those that can harm." As it turned out, the AI chatbot advised landlords that they could illegally discriminate against tenants on rental assistance, told restaurant and bar owners they could illegally take a cut of their workers' tips, told funeral home operators they could illegally conceal their prices, and told retail operators they could go cashless despite a legal requirement since 2020 in NYC to accept cash payments. Whoops.

McDonald's & IBM Consulting have a drive-through fiasco.

McDonald's announced in June 2024 that it was ending a 3-year project with IBM consulting to deploy AI to take drive-through orders. This was after hundreds of annoyed customers posted videos on social media as they tried in vain to get the AI to understand what they wanted to order. A now infamous TikTok video[6] showed two customers repeatedly trying to get the AI to stop as it kept adding more orders for Chicken McNuggets, eventually ordering 260 portions. In other videos, the AI ordered nine iced teas for a customer instead of one, was stumped when asked why a Mountain Dew drink was unavailable, and thought another customer was ordering bacon to add to his ice cream. I dread to think how many millions of dollars were wasted.

Air Canada and the chatbot lies they tried to disown.

In February 2024, Air Canada was ordered to pay compensation to a customer (Jake Moffat) after a chatbot gave him misleading information on bereavement fares when he was booking a ticket after his grandmother passed away in November 2023. The chatbot told him to buy a full-fare ticket and apply for a bereavement discount within 90 days. But when he applied as instructed, the airline refused the application, citing a policy that bereavement discounts could not be claimed on previously purchased tickets. Mr Moffat took the airline to a tribunal, claiming it was negligent in providing false information via its AI virtual assistant. In a beautiful example of corporate accountability, Air Canada argued that it "cannot be held liable for the information provided by the chatbot[7]". In summing up the decision to uphold Mr Moffat's complaint, Tribunal Member Christopher C. Rivers made the following observation: "Air Canada argues it cannot be held liable for information provided by one of its agents, servants, or representatives – including a chatbot. It does not explain why it believes that is the case. In effect, Air Canada suggests the chatbot is a separate legal entity that is responsible for its own actions. This is a remarkable submission. While a chatbot has an interactive component, it is still just a part of Air Canada's website. It should be obvious to Air Canada that it is responsible for all the information on its website. It makes no difference whether the information comes from a static page or a chatbot."

Sports Illustrated accused of misleadingly publishing content generated by fake AI authors.

In November 2023, the online magazine *Futurism* accused Sports Illustrated of publishing content by fake AI-generated authors[8]. They cited the example of an article purportedly by Drew Ortiz, whose author biography at Sports Illustrated[9] suggested he was entirely human:

"Drew likes to say that he grew up in the wild, which is partially true. He grew up in a farmhouse surrounded by woods, fields, and a creek. Drew has spent much of his life outdoors and is excited to guide you through his never-ending list of the best products to keep you from falling to the perils of nature. Nowadays, there is rarely a weekend goes by where Drew isn't out camping, hiking, or just back on his parents' farm".

However, *Futurism* noted that Drew didn't exist outside this profile. He had no presence on social media and no history of publishing articles in other publications. Furthermore, his profile photo was from a website that sold AI-generated images. The photo caption read: "neutral white young-adult male with short brown hair and blue eyes." After *Futurism* asked Sports Illustrated's publisher, Arena Group, to comment, Drew's article and others like it were taken down. Arena group stated that the articles in question "were product reviews and were licensed content from an external, third-party company, AdVon Commerce", saying, "We have learned that AdVon had writers use a pen or pseudo name in certain articles to protect author privacy - actions we don't condone - and we are removing the content while our internal investigation continues and have since ended the partnership." In response *Futurism* said, "Our sources familiar with the creation of the content disagree." The whole fiasco did not go down well with the Sports Illustrated

Union, who issued the following statement: "If true, these practices violate everything we believe in about journalism. We deplore being associated with something so disrespectful to our readers."

iTutor Group's ageist recruiting AI debacle.

In August 2023, iTutor Group, a US-based online tutoring company, agreed to pay $365,000 to settle a lawsuit initiated by the US Equal Employment Opportunity Commission (EEOC). The lawsuit accused the company, which provides remote tutoring services to Chinese students, of using AI-powered recruiting software that automatically rejected female applicants over 55 and male applicants over 60. According to the EEOC, over 200 qualified applicants were rejected by the software on grounds of age. EEOC Chair Charlotte Burrows said: "Age discrimination is unjust and unlawful. Even when technology automates the discrimination, the employer is still responsible." iTutor Group denied any wrongdoing but agreed to settle and put in place strengthened anti-discrimination policies.

If you are still thinking of pressing ahead with AI replacing people, you may wish to consider the worst-case scenarios that will be conspicuously absent from the business case the consultants wrote for you.

HUMANITY OVER EFFICIENCY: REASONS TO BE HOPEFUL

What helps people helps business.

— LEO BURNETT

ALL PROGRESS DEPENDS ON THE UNREASONABLE

George Bernard Shaw, the Irish playwright, activist, and winner of the Nobel Prize for Literature, once observed that reasonable people adapt themselves to the world, whereas unreasonable people persist in trying to adapt the world to themselves. He concluded, therefore, that all progress depended on the unreasonable. To try and change the work belief system that is so embedded is the epitome of unreasonableness. But changing deeply embedded beliefs can be done – otherwise, we would all still think the Earth was flat. If enough people are unreasonable in demanding change, the path to shifting the collective belief system will emerge. But where do you start if you want to change your organisation? The following chapters will explore the areas where the evidence shows the most promise.

THE PRESSING NEED TO REINVENT HR

Human resources gets a lot of bad press, mostly well-deserved. The HR function annoys most employees and their managers, and its reputation seems to have noticeably gone downhill since the Covid-19 pandemic. That's when HR began to make up and police rules about remote working, launched many diversity, equity and inclusion initiatives and was basically behind everything else that has unsettled the workplace in the past four years. Unfortunately, in many organisations, HR has also become both an easy entry point for external nonsense and the unquestioning execution partner for internal nonsense. Often, HR takes the blame when it all unravels.

Despite all the talk about engagement, talent and 'employer value proposition', HR has been a massive disappointment as a profession and a function for decades. Executives working as HR professionals are probably even more annoyed at the state of HR than the rest of your organisation's employees. Research from LinkedIn in 2022 showed that HR had the highest turnover rate of any job function worldwide[1]. Hebba Youssef, the Chief People Officer at US organisation Workweek, runs a popular podcast for HR professionals called *I Hate it Here*[2]. Hebba describes HR as "one of the most soul-crushing industries to work in" and notes, "Everybody hates us." So, how can we shift the HR paradigm to one that adds more value and subtracts more nonsense? The answer may lie in two directions: examining the reason for HR's existence and moving to an evidence-based approach.

With most businesses now run by overly rational MBA types, there is a vital role for a function that genuinely focuses on humanity and acts to protect the company against the harm of nonsense and narrow efficiency perspectives. HR must step into this space and define a new reason to exist. The HR team could advocate for greater autonomy. They should challenge the nonsense of well-being, performance appraisals, half-baked DEI initiatives and engagement surveys. They must help the business find ways to kill other nonsense and uncover hidden talent.

Helpfully, much good thinking has already been done, if not widely adopted. The movement for Evidence-based HR has gathered pace in recent years, with some notable organisations formed to research and promote the practice, including the Center for Evidence-Based Management (CEBMa), the Academy to Innovate HR (AIHR), and the Corporate Research Forum (CRF). The CIPD has this to say about the need to be more evidence-based:

"Within the people profession, we face a barrage of often contradictory insights and wild claims about what works in organisations and what doesn't. In addition, every couple of years, large international consulting firms promote a new, cutting-edge model or solution that promises to empower your employees and boost your organisation's performance. Especially in a 'post-truth' era."

In his book *The Organized Mind*[3], neuroscientist Daniel Levin writes about the challenge of information overload in modern societies. According to Daniel, "We're assaulted with facts, pseudo facts, jibber-jabber, and rumour, all posing as information. Trying to figure out what you need to know and what you can ignore is exhausting." In the face of this information onslaught, we tend to fall back on heuristics, mental shortcuts, to help us make decisions. Unfortunately, these mental shortcuts leave us highly prone to biases. Common biases we see playing out in the HR function include:

- *Conformity bias* - evident in the tendency to conform to senior executives' rational worldviews and copy practices widespread in other HR functions. The engagement survey is an excellent example of conformity bias in action, the unthinking comfort of the herd.
- *Authority Bias* - the tendency to over-value or give more weight to views from organisations or individuals seen as authorities (think McKinsey or Simon Sinek as examples) and a reluctance to apply critical thinking to examine these views.
- *Confirmation Bias* - seeking evidence that supports existing beliefs and ignoring evidence to the contrary.

HR professionals and other managers seem woefully unaware that a wealth of good and easily accessible academic research exists that would help them to critically review the opinions of consultants and 'gurus' and the nonsense of outdated 'best practice'. In a study of managerial attitudes and perceived barriers regarding evidence-based practice[4], researchers surveyed 2,789 management practitioners in Belgium, the Netherlands, the United States, the United Kingdom and Australia. The findings were stark:

"Most respondents report basing their decisions on personal experience (91%), intuition (64%), knowledge acquired through formal education (62%), advice from colleagues (59%), insights provided by experts (56%) or management literature (34%). Only a minority indicated that they often base their decisions on findings from scientific research (27%), and an even smaller minority (14%) had ever read a peer-reviewed academic journal." This has to change. The CEBMa defines evidence-based practice as:

"Making decisions through the conscientious, explicit and judicious use of the best available evidence from multiple sources... to increase the likelihood of a favourable outcome."

Conscientious means genuinely seeking and using evidence from multiple sources – not just opinions or so-called 'best practice'. Explicit means you take a systematic, transparent, and reproducible approach – describing how you acquired the evidence and evaluated its quality. In addition, to prevent cherry-picking, you must explicitly define the criteria you used to select the evidence. Judicious, in this context, means critically appraised.

Being evidence-based does not mean looking for absolute proof - complexity is too tricky. However, we can and should prioritise the most trustworthy evidence available and stop all the nonsense without an evidence base. The upsides of making better decisions and becoming genuinely value-adding are significant for HR as a profession and a function and vital for releasing organisations from much nonsense.

29

THE IMPORTANCE OF CRITICAL THINKING

We are primarily in this unenviable situation at work due to a spectacular lack of critical thinking. As we've seen throughout this book, most of the misguided elements of our work-life belief systems crumble under the slightest glance of critical review. Belief perseverance can't be cured by critical thinking alone, but the ability and willingness to question accepted wisdom has a place along the path to more meaningful change. This is particularly so in the corporate version of 'defence against the dark arts*', i.e., defending against pseudoscience research published by management consultants and others.

As discussed earlier, unlike the research published by career academics, research from consulting firms is typically not peer-reviewed or published in respected journals. Careers are not at risk for spurious claims; the opposite seems true. This research is often completely biased, entirely conflicted and poorly constructed. In my view, every senior manager and executive should be trained in critically reviewing this kind of marketing

---

* For any Harry Potter fans

dressed up as research instead of just unquestioningly accepting it and using it to justify spurious initiatives (no matter how well intended). At a very minimum, any research that's being cited to justify an investment or intervention should go through a basic set of questions:

1. *Who did the research?* Academics or a bunch of junior management consultants? If it was academics, what other papers have they published? How many times have they been cited?
2. *Was the research peer-reviewed and published* in a respected independent publication?
3. *Is there evidence of bias in the starting assumptions?* For example, research papers starting with a sentence like "Culture is the primary determinant of performance..." or other biased and silly entry points should be ignored entirely.
4. *What methodology was deployed?* Hint: Any methodology that includes analysing earnings calls or annual reports, relying on self-reported data, cherry-picking organisations to include, etc., should be immediately treated with suspicion.
5. *Is there any evidence that indicates causation and not just correlation?* Would the reverse hypothesis be just as valid a conclusion? For example, does higher employee engagement make companies successful, or could working for already successful companies make higher engagement more likely? In a complex world, how likely is it that one variable can be isolated from the multitude of others?
6. *Who stands to gain from this research?* Where are the conflicts of interest? Who funded the study? What are we being sold?

7. *Does other published independent research support or
   contradict* these findings?

More broadly, CEOs and executives should mandate that any proposed HR-related investment based on 'best practice' or 'accepted wisdom' will be examined for evidence that the proposed approach is worth testing.

In the unlikely (but highly desirable) situation that an employee proposes an entirely novel and untested practice, CEOs should briefly pause to celebrate an original idea mysteriously appearing in a sea of conformity. Then, they should challenge their teams to construct a series of small experiments to test the idea, maybe even in partnership with an academic whose interest area converges. That would be something worth celebrating, regardless of the outcomes.

To support and assess levels of critical thinking, there are a number of helpful academic models of cognitive processes. The best-known of these is Bloom's Taxonomy (revised 2001)[1]. In this model, cognitive processes are arranged and described in order, starting with 'remember' and progressing to 'create'. The six levels are:

1. *Remember* (recall facts and basic concepts)
2. *Understand* (explain ideas or concepts)
3. *Apply* (use information in new situations)
4. *Analyse* (draw connections among ideas)
5. *Evaluate* (justify a stand or decision)
6. *Create* (produce new or original work)

Most teams I have encountered in organisations operate at levels 1-3. Ways to encourage better thinking at the team level include *Pre-mortems* (which we explored in Chapter 17), *Planned Disagreements* (setting the expectations of finding reasons to argue against a course of action), and combining *Idea Generation* with *Idea Evaluation* into team meeting agendas. Another starting point for broader individual critical thinking might be to explore the themes in this book in more depth, doing your own research to seek answers to questions such as:

- What can I learn about the exceptions, the mavericks, the ones who've abandoned 'best practice' in the search for original practice?
- How can I surface and challenge my biases and most deeply held beliefs about life at work?
- What's the latest thinking emerging from diverse fields such as neuroscience, behavioural economics, social science, psychology, technology, etc., and what might some of the implications be?

A word of warning: once you start on this path, it may be hard to stop. But that's no bad thing.

Top-down authority structures turn employees into bootlickers, breed pointless struggles for political advantage, and discourage dissent.

— GARY HAMEL

30

THE CASE FOR GREATER AUTONOMY

We've seen that allowing individuals to have too much or too little power predicts many adverse outcomes. Powerful individuals become more detached, less caring, overconfident, and prone to bad behaviour. At the same time, leaving individuals powerless creates demotivation and low self-esteem and impacts wellbeing. Without some autonomy, we fundamentally suppress the talent and creativity of our employees.

The *2023 Future of Jobs Report*[1] issued by the World Economic Forum shows that creative thinking was the second most crucial core skill for employees identified by the respondent organisations. Over 73% (net) considered this skill to be of rising importance (the highest score of any skill in the dataset). Interestingly, the same organisations estimated that, on average, less than 7% of employees demonstrated creative thinking skills. I believe this glaring disparity has far less to do with innate talent and far more to do with limited autonomy.

We have evidence that autonomy increases motivation, reduces stress, improves well-being, makes jobs more interesting, and fosters creativity. Yet, we maintain the status quo. If we never allow people to apply creative thinking to their work, why are we surprised to see so little evidence of it in our organisations? It's the system, not the individuals.

Could a focus on creating more autonomy throughout the organisation help with all these issues? If you remember our discussion on wellbeing early in the book, researchers found that the typical wellbeing interventions deployed by most organisations had no effect. The only intervention shown to have an impact was training managers to support their employees' autonomy more. This led to employees reporting greater job satisfaction, improved wellbeing and more positive and trusting attitudes to top management. In addition to conferring many other benefits, increased autonomy positively changes employees' perceptions of the organisation.

In his book *The Decision Maker: Unlock the Potential of Everyone in Your Organization, One Decision at a Time*[2], CEO Dennis Bakke tells a fable based on his experiments to genuinely devolve decision-making throughout AES, a global power company with 27,000 employees. In a strikingly similar argument to that articulated by Kandiaronk, the eloquent Wendat statesman we met in Chapter 11, Dennis maintains that the ability to make decisions is central to the fundamental nature of being human.

We have evolved to have the innate ability to think, reason, make decisions and hold ourselves accountable. We constantly make decisions in our personal lives, but at work, most of us are expected just blindly to follow instructions rather than use our highly developed decision-making skills. Dennis says: "Creating an environment that pushes decision-making down to the people closest to the action is best for the organisation, and it's even more important for the individuals that make up that organisation."

He describes an elegant decision-making process in which

an employee knowledgeable about the topic takes ownership of a decision. To arrive at the decision, they must seek advice and counsel from their peers and senior leaders – but the decision is theirs to make having done so. Interestingly, Netflix's current thinking[3] on decision-making is remarkably similar:

"We avoid decision-making by committee, which tends to slow companies down and undermine accountability. For every significant decision, we identify an informed captain who's responsible for making a judgment call on the right way ahead."

This opportunity to have autonomy, make progress and feel a sense of purpose mirrors the findings of Dan Pink's research published in *Drive: The Surprising Truth About What Really Motivates Us*. Dan's review of *The Decision Maker* concludes: "Dennis Bakke brings these principles to life in a modern business fable with ample lessons for building successful organisations from the ground up."

But could increasing autonomy throughout the organisation also mitigate the undesirable side effects of too much power residing in a small number of individuals? By creating ways to devolve power, we might get a double bang for our buck. It's an intriguing possibility. I'm much more drawn to testing this approach than the suggested mitigations against the corruption of power outlined in the *Harvard Business Review*[4]. In their article, the authors suggest that "seeking opportunities to show compassion" and "doing a daily compassion meditation" might save leaders from succumbing to the corrupting effects of power. I suspect that's pretty unlikely. We can and should do much more.

Taking the concepts of autonomy even further takes us into the world of self-managing teams and flattened hierarchies, described by the author Frédéric Laloux in his book *Reinventing Organizations*. One of the organisations featured in the book, Buurtzorg, has become a poster child for high autonomy and low hierarchy organisation design. It was founded in the Netherlands in 2006 by Jos de Blok and a small team of professional nurses who realised that years of organisational nonsense and narrow, rational, efficiency-driven changes had undermined their relationships with patients. They set out to simplify the healthcare system and demonstrate a genuinely patient-centred way of working.

Along the way, they created high autonomy for the nursing teams and their clients, whom they recognised wanted to have control over their own lives and live independently for as long as possible. They describe their philosophy for self-managing clients:

"The professional attunes to the client and their context, taking into account the living environment, the people around the client, a partner or relative at home, and on into the client's informal network; their friends, family, neighbours and clubs as well as professionals already known to the client in their formal network. In this way the professional seeks to build a solution involving the client and their formal and informal networks. Self-management, continuity, building trusting relationships, and building networks in the neighbourhood are all important and logical principles for the teams."

The results have been spectacular. Following the 'Humanity Over Bureaucracy' principle, Buurtzorg has grown to over 950 self-managed nursing teams, employing over 15,000 nurses. The business has been voted Employer of the Year in The Netherlands four out of the last five years. Employee satisfaction is at 87%[5]. Productivity is so high that an independent assessment by EY showed that this approach generated savings of over 40% for the Dutch healthcare system. In 2016, Buurtzorg used its approach to transform two competing Dutch care companies. Both are now enjoying similar gains in productivity and staff and client satisfaction.

In 2009, the executive team at Netflix wrote an internal slide deck entitled "Freedom & Responsibility Culture." Subsequently, it went viral, with over 5 million online views. Former Facebook COO Sheryl Sandberg called it "One of the most important documents ever to come out of Silicon Valley". Autonomy was a central theme throughout the document, which included statements such as:

- *Responsible people thrive on freedom and are worthy of freedom.*
- *Our model is to increase employee freedom as we grow rather than limit it.*
- *We try to get rid of rules where we can to reinforce the point*.*
- *Netflix's policy for expenses, entertainment, gifts & travel: Act in Netflix's best interests (5 words).*
- *Formalised development is rarely effective, and we don't try to do it. Individuals should manage their own career paths.*

Netflix continues to adapt and refine these practices today, advocating for *People over Process*[6]:

"Many of us have worked at companies where decisions were made top down, there was little transparency, and it felt hard to make a difference — or even get basic things done. At Netflix, we aim to inspire and empower more than just manage because people can have a greater impact when they're free to make decisions about their own work."

Meanwhile, despite growing evidence that alternative organ-

---

* Netflix famously scrapped the vacation policy and tracking. Patty McCord, the company's Chief Talent Officer, remarked, "There is also no clothing policy at Netflix, but no one has come to work naked lately."

isational constructs can deliver exceptional results, 99.99% of large organisations carry on unquestioningly with the old models and all the nonsense they entail. I'm not suggesting that all large organisations immediately move to dissolve their hierarchies – that would probably cause untold chaos. However, there are easy, practical, and low-cost ways to test whether changing power distribution is beneficial. The first is *increasing autonomy from the bottom up*. This has two components:

1. Training frontline and middle managers to support greater autonomy for the teams they lead[7].
2. Providing those teams with the time and design tools to give them more control over their work and how the team's objectives are reached.

For example, in his book *Holacracy: The New Management System for a Rapidly Changing World*[8], Brian Robertson, CEO of a US software company, outlines a system his company uses to create highly autonomous teams. This system includes replacing rigid job titles and descriptions with 'roles' defined collectively at the team level. This means employees may take on multiple roles, each with specific decision-making rights and authority. Furthermore, roles can be traded between team members, so long as somebody does all the roles required for the team to meet its objectives. This allows team members to have far more control over their work, to learn and test out new roles, and to swap roles with other team members based on collective responsibility and collaboration.

The second is *devolving power from the top down*. This potentially has three components:

1. Educating executives and senior leaders on the effects of power and status on them as individuals,

finding ways to support greater empathy and critical examination of their belief systems. This could include coaching using the concept of 'Deep Canvassing'*, a fascinating conversational technique that has emerged from US voter canvassing.

2. Testing ways to increase co-determination, such as worker representatives on the executive committee and board.

3. Genuinely delegating decisions to those closer to the action, perhaps using the process outlined by Dennis Bakke or an alternative design concept.

Whatever way you look at it, increasing autonomy seems like a promising hypothesis to test.

---

* The *New Conversation Initiative*, an organisation that supports deep canvassing campaigns describes the technique: "Deep canvassing is about working to create mutual understanding grounded in lived experience, instead of in debate or talking points. When we take this approach, people's experience leads them away from prejudice, stigma, or fear, and towards empathy and a willingness to consider progressive solutions."

Not everything that can be counted counts, and not everything that counts can be counted.

— ALBERT EINSTEIN

31

LESS RATIONALITY, MORE MAGIC

Shinkansen is the Japanese name for the famous high-speed bullet trains that travel at 320 km/h across a network of nearly 3,000 miles. Tessei is the cleaning company that services the trains in Tokyo. Each bullet train stops at the station for 12 minutes. Allowing 5 minutes for embarking and disembarking leaves just 7 minutes to clean the entire train.

By 2005, Tessei's organisation in Tokyo struggled with low morale, high turnover, poor performance and an increasing number of accidents. They were hit with rising performance penalties, and income had dropped by over 20% since 2001 despite a 20% increase in work volume. Management consultants had completed 'time & motion' studies and standardised all processes and equipment in the rational pursuit of greater efficiency, but this only seemed to make things worse. The cleaning staff were demoralised and tried to remain as invisible as possible to the passengers as they did their work. Quotes from the staff at the time indicate that they had to endure customers openly pointing them out to their children as a 'warning' to succeed at school or end up 'like them'.

In 2005, Teruo Yabe was given the role of leading the Tokyo operation for Tessai. After observing the cleaning staff at work, he was mesmerised by the precision and speed at which some of the team worked. He had a radical idea. Instead of an invisible, low-status, demeaning cleaning job – he would reframe the activity into a highly visible, highly choreographed performance art, making it a central part of the Shinkansen experience.

Although the staff had some initial misgivings, Yabe worked with them to design bright, attractive uniforms and equipment to make them visible. On the arrival of each train, the staff would form a line on the platform and were asked to make eye contact with the passengers as they thanked them for taking their rubbish with them. This dramatically reduced the volumes of rubbish left on board (an early example of what became known as the Nudge Theory in behavioural economics).

As the staff got into the performance mindset, interesting things happened. Morale rocketed, accidents decreased, and performance was transformed. The team started to feel pride in their work, and people noticed. Customer videos of the ballet-like performance of high-speed cleaning went viral and were featured on Japanese TV and CNN. Now, people go to Tokyo station just to see the cleaners in action. They've become a tourist attraction. After each train is cleaned, the performance is applauded by onlookers and passengers. It's a magical transformation. The interesting thing about this story is that rational performance improvement techniques had no impact. Magic was created by changing the perception of the job, not the job itself. There's no way to write a business case for an intervention like this because it's entirely, joyfully, irrational.

As any good branding agency will tell you – perception is reality. Yet, in addressing business performance, we pay almost no attention to perception or creative ways to change it. This is hardly surprising when management education and management consultancies place far more emphasis and value on rational, analytical skills than on creative genius. Despite changing the structure, processes or technology, could success be fundamentally limited unless the perception of the employees and customers changes as well? Even more thought-provoking is the idea that we could get more bang for our buck by focusing solely on changing perception, avoiding all the potentially unnecessary expense and upheaval of changing all that other stuff.

A few years ago, I had the opportunity to observe a fascinating experiment that completely changed the way an Irish insurance company worked without changing its structures, reporting lines, or job descriptions. At the bottom of the company's hierarchy, customer service agents fielded calls from customers seeking insurance coverage. The requirements would then be passed up the line to various other specialist teams, underwriters, and, if complex enough, actuaries. Draft policies were frequently held up, leaving the agents dealing with annoyed customers as they searched for information about the delay. They often waited several days for a response from other departments.

Business process reengineering and 'Lean' initiatives had failed to solve the problem, so the CEO (Sean, a most interesting character) agreed to try something different. A cross-functional team came together to answer how long the ten or so most requested types of policy cover should take to process. Once that was agreed, the customer service agents were asked to change their language with the customer. They were to say: "I promise that your policy will be ready in X days" (depending on the complexity). As they passed the work up the line, each person was to make the next person in the chain aware of the promise. If, for any reason, the promise was unlikely to be kept, the person who had the work in progress had to call the customer directly and explain the situation.

This was a subtle but colossal shift. People at all levels suddenly found themselves talking to customers for the first time, even the actuaries who traditionally barely spoke to other humans. Strangely, they started to like it. They even began to call the customers to tell them everything was good and that the policy would be delivered as promised. Processing times dropped by over 50%, customer satisfaction rocketed, and employees reported significantly higher levels of job control and enhanced satisfaction—all from a subtle language change.

In both stories, an overly rational, efficiency-driven approach to solving the problems failed miserably before an irrational idea saved the day by reframing the situation and trying something entirely novel. Unfortunately, cases of novel thinking like this are incredibly rare in business. The rational spreadsheet monkeys rule the zoo. If someone proposes testing a left-field idea on a problem that's resisted all other approaches, you might be wise to listen, even if it initially sounds wild.

If you are in a senior leadership role, the next time you have a 'beauty parade' of consulting firms that pitch to help you solve a thorny business problem, why not put the brief out to some creative agencies as well? Through Design Thinking, you might discover an entirely different perspective. There's unlikely to be much downside, but it might be much more fun.

32

LESSONS FROM DESIGN THINKING

Design thinking comprises approaches to problem-solving that aim to overcome existing preconceptions and foster creativity to achieve innovative solutions. Largely ignored for decades outside the design community, design thinking became popular after Tim Brown, CEO and President of the global design firm IDEO, wrote an article about it in the *Harvard Business Review* in June 2008[1].

First, the approach involves profoundly understanding the problem and setting aside preconceptions and biases to examine it holistically. The second stage explores a wide range of potential solutions, and the third stage involves iterating extensively through prototyping and testing before finally implementing.

When it works, it can produce real magic. In 2007, the Danish municipality of Holstebro had a problem. It had a large population of senior citizens who relied on the delivery of government-sponsored free meals. Many of these senior citizens had nutritional challenges, resulting in health problems and burdening the municipality's health and social services. Holstebro applied for a program offered through the Danish Enterprise and Construction Authority that funds partnerships between cities and Danish design firms. The design firm Hatch & Bloom signed on to improve the outcomes of the meal service. At the outset, everybody assumed the project would result in menu changes based on updated customer preferences and nutritional improvements. However, the design approach led in a completely unexpected direction, with interesting similarities to the Shinkansen story we met in the last chapter.

The Hatch & Bloom team used an ethnographic* research process focused on understanding the existing situation and unarticulated needs. They rode with delivery drivers, entered the customers' homes, and watched what happened as meals were consumed. However, it was a visit to the public kitchens that helped the team to reframe the problem. In a similar situation to the train cleaners we met in Tokyo, working in a public kitchen was a low-status job in Denmark. There seemed to be a perception that people who worked in these public kitchens were lazy and unskilled and that the kitchens were poorly run. Employees were demoralised. Because of a focus on efficiency and process, the same menus were produced daily, only changing once every three months. This was highly dull for both the employees and the customers. There was no opportunity to be creative or innovative.

A visit from a well-known chef led to surprising conclusions. His view was that the employees had skills comparable to professional chefs but were forced to behave more like unskilled workers on a factory production line. Little attention was paid to presentation, seasoning or even the language used on the menu to describe the dishes. Back on the customer side, meals were delivered in battered, dirty vehicles. This reinforced issues with

---

* Ethnographic research is a method used to study the behaviours, beliefs, and social interactions of a particular group. It involves directly observing, and participating in, daily life and the activities of the group being researched.

the social stigma that customers felt in accepting the meal service. They had little opportunity for feedback and experienced low autonomy, having little choice or input into the menus.

The design team realised that changing the perception of both employees and customers could be the key to unlocking a much better experience for all. They set about testing a series of interventions. The service was rebranded and changed from 'Hospitable Food Service' to 'The Good Kitchen'. Staff in the kitchens were given chef uniforms. Menus were altered to look and read like high-quality restaurant menus, with mouth-watering descriptions of the food. Kitchen teams were encouraged to focus on the presentation. Dishes were redesigned with input from customers and staff, including options like menus for two if a visitor was coming and more choices on individual snacks.

Drivers were given feedback cards and encouraged to solicit customer suggestions for improving the service. Photos from customers' homes were displayed in the kitchens to help the team feel closer to the customers. The Good Kitchen also began publishing a newsletter for customers that introduced the kitchen teams and updated them on ideas and feedback. And it worked. When the new menus were launched, orders rose by 500% in the first week. Rather than struggling to recruit staff, the number of unsolicited job applications shot up. The Good Kitchen and Hatch & Bloom shared the *Danish Design Prize for Service Design*, as well as the *Local Government Denmark Prize for Innovation* in 2009.

Based on this and many other documented successes of the design thinking approach[2], many large organisations began efforts to adopt design thinking. However, very few went on to achieve the magical changes illustrated by the Shinkansen story or The Good Kitchen. So, what went wrong? Bruce Nussbaum is a former Assistant Managing Editor for *Business Week* and a Professor of Innovation and Design at Parsons School of Design. He was one of the early advocates for the adoption of Design Thinking. Writing in Fast Company magazine, he suggests that design consultancies packaged the Design Thinking approach as a 'process' to appeal to the world of big business, which he viewed as defined by an obsession with process efficiency (which, as we know, generally kills all joy and magic). Having a 'process' made it easier to sell creativity to big corporations and their rationality-loving CEOs. In his view, companies took to the process side of the approach a little too well, turning the concept of Design Thinking into a linear, time-bound, project-managed methodology that unsurprisingly produced often mediocre results.

IDEO's Tim Brown, whose HBR article had kickstarted the broader adoption of Design Thinking, had a similar reflection. He noted that the Design Thinking process downplayed the 'messy' nature of the iterative reality of design, with all its emotions, false starts, conflicts and failures. In his view, only a few companies and CEOs accepted this messy reality and achieved real innovation. Most simply did not, abandoning Design Thinking when their more 'rational' version of the process failed to achieve any breakthroughs. Organisations seemed reluctant to accept one of design thinking's key features —that the problem you might solve is not the same one you initially set out to solve. Changing the scope was often seen as a failure rather than a valid and valuable outcome. It appears that pretending there is a rational, linear, and predictable process for finding magic is unlikely to succeed. However, ample evidence suggests that design thinking can produce brilliant results if given the space to do so.

33

CLOSING THE DOOR ON THE BIG 4

The Big 4's consulting businesses essentially operate a legal pyramid scheme. The base of the pyramid consists of inexperienced graduates hired out for client projects at eye-watering day rates. The profits are rolled up to the top, where the partners feed off the spoils. As a result, partners earn 15-20 times the pay of those who do the actual work. It's an epic cash-generating machine. Many partners will take senior executive roles in industry, where they prop the door open for their old mates, and the merry-go-round continues.

One good thing about bringing consultants into your business is that, unlike your already frazzled employees, they have the luxury of the capacity to focus on solving an issue without the constant demands of the day job. They are also typically able to be more objective than employees, who are always conscious of hierarchy and the consequences of making their sometimes inept managers look bad.

The downsides of hiring consultants include a complete lack of knowledge about your business (and often the industry), no understanding of how informal networks operate in your organisation, and the fact that they look and sound like strange cult members to most of your employees, who struggle to relate to them.

But suppose you could have all the advantages without the disadvantages and for 1/10th of the cost? You can. It's called growing your own. Here's how it works:

1. Commit to a 12-month experiment to create a small internal team (perhaps 4-5 employees) to work on important opportunities and issues across the business.
2. Put aside any preconceptions about the need for prior experience, seniority, formal qualifications, location, job role, etc.
3. Encourage applications from across the business, regardless of role or length of service. Think about how to make the application process fun and use it as an opportunity to let people demonstrate creative thinking.
4. Put the team under the wing of a senior executive, ensuring they are entirely outside the reporting line of operations and HR. Strategy or Finance could be choices for a home, but the team needs to report directly to the executive.
5. Spend a month training the team in critical thinking, complexity, design thinking, hypothesis development and testing, and basic data analytics. Send them to visit interesting businesses in other sectors and geographies.
6. Consider how to generate 'pull' from the business to pitch for the team to come and work on intractable problems or interesting opportunities in different areas.

7. See what happens. Learn from the first foray, iterate and go again.

Based on experience doing this, the 12-month project will cost roughly the same as 4-6 weeks of a consulting project with a similar-sized team. But it could deliver so much more, and you get to keep the team afterwards. It could also help uncover your organisation's hidden talent and signal to your people that there are other, more interesting career paths than the traditional corporate ladder. This is real inclusion in action.

When implementing good ideas, an internal team like this has the advantage of an existing network and the relatability of being "people like us" for your frontline teams. If you choose to test this idea, I predict you will be blown away by the hidden talent you uncover.

The power of accurate observation is commonly called cynicism by those who have not got it.

— GEORGE BERNARD SHAW

34

HOW DEEP DOES IT GO? THE NONSENSE AUDIT

Understanding how deeply nonsense is embedded in your organisation is a sensible starting point for freeing your employees from as much nonsense as possible. Imagine the boost to productivity and happiness—not to mention general relief! Understanding the whole picture will require good ethnographic research to explore the obvious and not-so-obvious consequences of waste, frustration, and annoyance for employees and customers. Done well, this should prove highly illuminating and bring some unexpected insights. However, as a first step, the following articulations of nonsense levels may prove to be a useful, if not exhaustive, starting point.

Corporate Vision

- **Level 1.** The vision is relatively abstract and focused on the as-is (e.g. to be the "leading" or "best" something or other).
- **Level 2.** The vision includes delusional aspirations of great innovation, game-changing, etc., entirely unrelated to current capabilities.

- **Level 3** The vision arguably fundamentally opposes the company's business model and actual practices (e.g., Unilever).

Values & Purpose

- **Level 1.** They exist but are broadly standalone - nobody pays too much attention to them except the HR team.
- **Level 2.** Values and purpose are heavily featured in strategic plans, business cases, job descriptions, and other documents. Many trinkets adorned with the values have been distributed to the masses.
- **Level 3.** Values and purpose are embedded in behavioural frameworks, performance appraisals and recruitment/promotion criteria, creating an industry of annoying and pointless nonsense.

Culture

- **Level 1.** The executive team and board hold 'culture reviews', possibly with external 'culture experts' in support.
- **Level 2.** As per level 1 plus, one or more employees in HR have 'culture' in their job title. There may be evidence of employee 'culture' forums or discussion groups.
- **Level 3.** As per level 2, with a 'culture change' programme underway across some or all of the organisation. There may be a senior HR role dedicated to culture.

Artificial Intelligence

- **Level 1.** Executives have started talking about AI in board presentations and analyst conversations but haven't done anything silly yet. Management consultants are still trying to get a foothold.
- **Level 2.** One or more AI pilots have been launched without much intelligent consideration. High consulting fees are already being paid. Business cases are based on narrow and extremely rational logic. Outcomes are unclear as yet.
- **Level 3.** A multi-year AI partnership with a management consultancy has been agreed upon, with ambitious efficiency aims. In the unlikely event of achieving the aims, many years of savings will be required to pay the consulting fees and technology licences. Worst-case scenarios have not been considered. The organisation is carrying unknown risks. You should be afraid.

Performance Appraisals

- **Level 1.** Mandated for all employees, mainly manager-determined with some 360-degree input or similar.
- **Level 2.** Appraisals and targets/objectives are linked to financial incentives, leaving the system open to canvassing and gaming. To complicate matters further, HR has dedicated Rewards and Incentives staff.
- **Level 3.** As per level 2, with the addition of ridiculous requirements for evidence of 'living the values' to be documented in the appraisal process or promotion criteria.

Employee Engagement Surveys

- **Level 1.** An annual survey is administered, and results are shared without too much 'stuff' arising. Scores are linked to executive remuneration.
- **Level 2.** Surveys may be more frequent with the possible addition of smaller, more frequent 'pulse' type surveys. Scores linked to financial incentives for managers & executives. There are dedicated Employee Engagement staff in HR.
- **Level 3.** As per level 2, with the addition of 'listening sessions', workshops and action plans driving largely futile nonsense from the survey results.

Diversity, Equity & Inclusion

- **Level 1.** Diversity policies exist, with voluntary Unconscious Bias Training (UBT) on offer and limited activities lacking evidence-based outcomes.
- **Level 2.** As per level 1, with the addition of mandatory UBT training and rigid numerical targets for diversity in recruitment, management, etc. There are dedicated DEI staff in HR.
- **Level 3.** As per level 2 with a Chief Diversity Officer in post with the DEI team. A wide array of initiatives with no evidence base for outcomes. Diversity targets are linked to financial incentives for executives, raising the risks of unethical or illegal activity.

E in ESG

- **Level 1.** Environmental policies are in place but have vague plans and a high reliance on offsetting.

- **Level 2.** There is some evidence of greenwashing with eco slogans, branding or gaming of accreditations.
- **Level 3.** Significant nonsense and greenwashing are evident throughout branding, marketing and PR.

Wellbeing

- **Level 1.** Wellbeing policies are in place. The focus is email communication, signposting to external mental health providers, and other symbolic activities.
- **Level 2.** Dedicated wellbeing staff in HR. Several initiatives focused on the classics: mindfulness lessons or apps, stress & resilience training, etc.
- **Level 3.** Individuals are offered many initiatives (e.g., life coaching, dog-petting, soundwave healing, etc.). Multiple dedicated well-being staff members, possibly even a Chief Well-Being Officer, are employed.

Meetings

- **Level 1.** Executives and managers spend over 50% of their time in pre-scheduled meetings. There is no evidence of fun or enjoyment. Few decisions are made in the meetings.
- **Level 2.** Executives and managers spend over 60% of their time in meetings. There is evidence of boredom and distraction. Few meetings make any decisions. Many attendees find excuses to attend virtually, where they can surreptitiously scroll through social media on their out-of-view phones. Some evidence of surface acting.

- **Level 3.** Executives and managers spend over 70% of their time in meetings. Some of this time is used to "cascade" decisions they made before the meeting to compliant lackeys in middle management. Surface acting is prevalent and ensures no real dissent, even when it is well-known among attendees that the decision is sub-optimal. Many excuses are made to avoid attendance. Joy is conspicuously absent.

Change Management

- **Level 1.** Employees involved in change initiatives are selected for change management training and expected to follow a recognised 'change management framework'.
- **Level 2.** As per level 1, with the addition of a *Project Management Office* to apply 'change frameworks' across all projects. There may be one or more Change Manager roles in the organisation.
- **Level 3.** The organisation has a dedicated change team that is separate from the operational business. A senior role may be badged as *Director of Change* or *Transformation Director*. There is widespread evidence of attempts to predetermine the output of change initiatives. There is little evidence of successfully achieving the prescribed outcomes (except by gaming the results - the "everything is green on the update" fallacy).

Undertaking this audit exercise should highlight areas for deeper investigation. The conversations prompted should undoubtedly be enjoyable.

Every organisation should tolerate rebels who tell the emperor he has no clothes.

— COLIN POWELL

35

CONCLUDING THOUGHTS

I hope reading this book has given you a broader perspective on the nature of work and nonsense as most of us experience it. You may even feel inspired to test possible system interventions in your organisation. Given the nature of complex systems, different things might work in different contexts, but it is helpful to have a starting set of hypotheses to test, probe the system, and see what happens.

Most of us work in very hierarchical organisational structures. Unless you are in a high-status role, you may feel you have limited power to make any interventions, however small. But this would be a severely self-limiting belief. Author and social activist Alice Walker, the first African American woman to win the Pulitzer Prize for fiction, once said: "The most common way people give up their power is by thinking they don't have any".

Barry Oshry, the renowned systems thinker, spoke of the power of those experiencing the 'bottom' condition as 'fixers' who solve problems and inform those further up the hierarchy. Given the number of employees and proximity to customers, collective power is potentially enormous at the frontline. Directly engaging on your ideas with those at the top may be a better route than hoping your ideas filter upwards through the layers of hierarchy. There's little downside to trying something different.

You already control some resources if you are in a middle management role. Oshry describes the opportunity here as being an 'integrator', working with others in the middle layer to share information, coordinate functions, and move resources where needed to test new ideas. You don't need permission; just step into the opportunity. You may be surprised at the outcomes. As the Dalai Lama once said, "If you think you are too small to make a difference, try sleeping with a mosquito."

If nothing else, embarking on these journeys might bring curiosity, fun, and learning into the unnecessarily dull and conforming nature of organisations where many of us work. I hope you will be inspired to develop more ideas as you experiment. Check in on what's happening at the Sense Labs website (www.senselabs.co). New material will be added regularly, and you'll have the opportunity to share ideas with like-minded others.

Finally, given the massive concentration of power in the traditional hierarchy, the most significant opportunity for rapid system change in most contexts comes from the top. That's why, overleaf, I've penned an open letter to CEOs, suggesting some interventions entirely within their gift if they wish to challenge the conformity that is the default condition. I remain hopeful that CEOs will have the desire and interest to improve their legacy and leave behind a more capable and human organisation than they inherited—one with much less nonsense getting in the way of progress.

A GOOD PLACE TO END? AN OPEN LETTER TO THE CEO

So long as your desire to explore is greater than your
desire to not screw up, you're on the right track.

— ED HELMS

36

DEAR CEO

The bad news is that your organisation is highly dysfunctional, and your employees are inundated with nonsense. The good news is that your organisation is far from unique. The only question is: are you content with this situation? If not, the following paragraphs suggest some areas to consider experimenting with, although they are far from an exhaustive list of possibilities.

On Power & Autonomy

Challenge the tendency to blame culture for issues far more likely to be related to power and hierarchy. Educate your team on the dark sides of power. You and other executives are not immune. You are just human, like the rest of us. Understand that you are likely to become increasingly detached from the everyday reality of the worker. Consider ways to become less detached, including reverse mentoring, worker representation on the board, spending more time with frontline employees and customers, etc.

Genuinely devolving power down the hierarchy may be the

best way to reduce the adverse effects of power on leaders while boosting employee confidence, job satisfaction, and well-being. Enough evidence justifies a strong focus on autonomy throughout the organisation. It may be worth testing both top-down devolution of decision-making and bottom-up efforts to encourage greater autonomy.

On Critical Thinking

Understand our human tendency for *aversion to uncertainty*, *drive for sense-making* and *belief perseverance*. Don't let management consultants and content-light gurus evade your leadership team's bullshit filters. Encourage your team to do their research. Dismiss 'success' books that claim to have discovered 'secrets' or 'universal laws'. It's all complete rubbish.

Encourage your board of directors to think critically about governance and stop unquestioningly following a remarkably ineffective model. Tell them you expect more. Abandon the lazy and inept "board effectiveness" assessments in favour of something more likely to encourage adding genuine value.

Reframe HR's role to a focus on humanity and protecting the company against the harm of nonsense 'best practice' and narrow efficiency perspectives. Demand an evidence-based approach to decision-making.

If you have a leadership development programme, it's almost certainly teaching your leaders the wrong things. Either stop it or refocus your efforts on teaching them to be independent thinkers, support autonomy, deal with the dark sides of power, and embrace design thinking. Why not have them try to solve real problems in the organisation as a way of learning rather than debating 'heroic leadership' case studies in a classroom? If you want to use executive coaches, recommend the 'deep canvassing' method and ask them to help identify deeply held biases, blind spots, and beliefs that need to be challenged.

Consider cancelling 50% of your meetings—it probably doesn't matter which 50%. Use the time to get out, meet front-line employees and customers, and travel; you may find unexpected inspiration. Reframe key meetings as opportunities for genuine challenge and debate, testing ways to make them psychologically safer and reduce 'surface acting'. This may help avoid groupthink, bias, risk, and fake consensus for dumb ideas.

Don't assume past track record is predictive when you hire into the top team. Be particularly aware of incoming executives who, after a very short time, produce a 100-day plan or similar. It shows a complete lack of understanding of the importance of context. Task the headhunters you use to find more interesting people who demonstrate a capacity for curiosity and creative thinking, not just the usual suspects.

View any proposed restructuring with extreme suspicion. It will invariably be based on an oversimplified and rational view of how the organisation works and is far more likely to cause damage than create value. If you want to make changes, ask your employees for ideas and test them on a small scale first.

Rather than wasting money on management consultants, grow a small internal team to use a design-led approach to solving problems and pursuing new opportunities. This could be an exciting way to find hidden talent, test new approaches, and be more inclusive.

On Nonsense

You have an almost limitless opportunity to free your employees from nonsense. The more nonsense you eliminate, the more time your people will have to think and the more resources they will have to do something interesting.

Encourage your teams to have more time for thinking and less time in unproductive meetings. Thinking is work. If you are in the middle of a transformation programme or restructuring, bring the team together to discuss the lessons from complexity theory.

Ban the phrase 'living our values' and resist farcical efforts to 'measure' behaviour against them. Better still, abandon corporate values altogether; they have no demonstrable effect. Be honest about whether your business model can profitably deliver your purpose. If not, then rethink it or scrap it.

Beware of the high temptation to spin and greenwash your environmental ambitions like many others. Ask your teams for an honest assessment of progress and seek practical and credible ways to make a difference, even on a small scale.

Ditch your customer service training and the nonsense industry of service standards and manuals, and invest more in being careful who you hire to serve your customers.

Consider testing team-based incentives or removing incentives altogether and just paying people more. Also, consider testing the removal of performance appraisals or moving to more uncomplicated peer-based reviews, delinking appraisals from financial incentives.

Abandon the employee engagement survey and the industry of nonsense it generates. Instead, segment your employee base and do something original and valuable based on what you learn. Pull the plug on wellbeing efforts focused on individuals. The evidence is unequivocal that they have no effect. Critically examine DEI initiatives and training to see if they have positive and lasting outcomes. If not, stop. Instead, test batching recruitment and promotions to improve diversity. Adopting rigid targets for diversity may increase the risk of unethical or illegal behaviour, particularly if you link the targets to financial incentives. Aim not only for diversity in representation but also for diversity in thinking.

On Rationality, Artificial Intelligence & Human Magic

Remember that humans are, first and foremost, social animals. Our choices are driven far more by emotions and feelings than by rationality. Be careful about rational efficiency initiatives; their frames of reference are invariably blinkered. Organisation charts and job descriptions are incredibly poor proxies for the complexities of people's roles and impact.

Think long and hard about whether the employees the management consultants say you should replace with AI or any other technology have been allowed to think creatively or whether the system has created bland roles that deny that chance entirely. Ask yourself: what's missing in this picture? What might the unintended consequences be? Is there an opportunity to change perceptions and create new value? Beyond the narrow efficiency gains of replacing them with AI, will you kill the possibility of creating magical experiences that separate you from your competition?

Get a second opinion from a good design agency. A deeper understanding of context requires moving beyond the rational to emotions, behaviours, motivations, and unarticulated needs. The most valuable stage is exploration, where the space of possibility emerges. Resist pressure to rush past this to solutions.

Be aware of the dangers of the Turing Trap. If all that's left is AI, it's just a commodity. Worse still, it won't be yours to control; you'll depend on consultants and one or two big technology companies that will ultimately extract all the value. The risks are far higher than you've been led to believe. The technology is still emergent. Even the AI companies creating these models don't fully understand how they learn, let alone the management consultancies. Tread carefully, and don't be hypnotised by the hype.

With all their flaws, people are your best chance of creating something unique and interesting. Augmentation has more promise than automation and is undeniably more sustainable and responsible. It opens the possibility for genuine transformation. Automation creates incremental gains at best. Making something more efficient can make it worse for everyone; creating something more magical rarely results in a bad outcome for anyone.

On Exploring the Future

Abandon any illusions of predicting and controlling the future. This could be very liberating. The future will reveal itself through multiple small experiments. It's not a linear, predictable process of discovery. If your vision statement assumes that the future will be a slightly different version of today, then reflect on the infinitesimal chances of that being likely. Think about the underappreciated role of serendipity in business success and how you can increase its chances. Consider investing in exploring some interesting left-field ideas. Who knows where they might lead? Who needs a business case? We either want to invest in exploring the future, or we don't. No one ever wrote a business case for a significant breakthrough; they mostly happen by happy accident. Let's have some fun along the way. As Yoda said in *Star Wars*, "Do or not do. There is no try."

Sincerely yours etc.,

37

RESOURCES

For downloadable resources, recommended reading and discussions with like-minded explorers, please visit: www.senselabs.co

ACKNOWLEDGMENTS

To my wife Nicole, who supported my indulgence in writing this book, my children James, Isabella, Rafael and Luca, my brother Brendan, and my mother Valerie. Also, I want to thank the many people throughout my career who provided support, inspiration, challenge, and friendship. Richard Smith, Mark Palmer, Patrick Verwer, Mark Allan, Rob Hudson, Barry Oshry, Richard Simpson, Nick Hayes, James Hunt, Simon Jones and the strategy team at Unite, David Godber, Kit Jackson, Neill Whittaker, Nigel Carr, Craig Walker, Mark Baptist, Justin Grice, Darran Ling, Steve Davies, Chris Daniel, and many others. Thank you all. Thanks also to the great team at the Drop-In Work Club in Richmond, who are always ready with a friendly welcome and good coffee when serious writing time is required.

NOTES

1. NONSENSE & THE HUMAN CONDITION: EVOLUTIONARY HANGOVERS

1. Using Neuroscience to Help Understand Fear and Anxiety: A Two-System Framework, Joseph E. LeDoux Ph.D & Daniel S. Pine, M.D, American Journal of Psychiatry, Volume 173, Number 11
2. Computations of uncertainty mediate acute stress responses in humans, Nature Communications 7, Article number: 10996 (2016)
3. Perceived job insecurity and worker health in the United States, Sarah A. Burgard, Jennie E Brand, PhD, and James S House, PhD, Social Science & Medicine, Volume 69 Issue 5, September 2009
4. Boelen PA, Reijntjes A. Intolerance of uncertainty and social anxiety. J Anxiety Disord. 2009 Jan;23(1):130-5
5. The under-appreciated drive for sense-making, Journal of Economic Behavior & Organization, Volume 126 Part B, June 2016
6. https://en.wikipedia.org/wiki/List_of_creation_myths
7. https://en.wikipedia.org/wiki/Big_Bang
8. https://www.who.int/news-room/fact-sheets/detail/noncommunicable-diseases
9. Ultraprocessed food and chronic noncommunicable diseases: A systematic review and meta-analysis of 43 observational studies, Lane MM, Davis JA, Beattie S, Gómez-Donoso C, Loughman A, O'Neil A, Jacka F, Berk M, Page R, Marx W, Rocks T. Obesity Review. March 2021
10. Source: Precedence Research
11. https://www.who.int/tools/elena/interventions/fruit-vegetables-ncds
12. How Not to Die: Discover the Foods Scientifically Proven to Prevent and Reverse Disease, Dr Michael Greger MD & Gene Stone, Pan Books, December 2017
13. https://archive.nytimes.com/well.blogs.nytimes.com/2015/02/03/new-york-attorney-general-targets-supplements-at-major-retailers/
14. https://www.mayoclinic.org/drugs-supplements-vitamin-c/art-20363932
15. Enough is enough: Stop wasting money on vitamin and mineral supplements, Editorial: The Annals of Internal Medicine, January 2014
16. Broccoli: A Multi-Faceted Vegetable for Health: An In-Depth Review of Its Nutritional Attributes, Antimicrobial Abilities, and Anti-inflammatory Properties: Antibiotics (Basel), July 2023
17. https://www.nobelprize.org/prizes/medicine/2024/press-release/
18. When Prophecy Fails: A Social and Psychological Study of a Modern Group

That Predicted the Destruction of the World, Leon Festinger, Henry Riecken, Stanley Schachter, Harper-Torchbooks, January 1956

19. The Solar Star Command: https://www.star-essence.org
20. Jon D. Miller, Eugenie C. Scott, Mark S. Ackerman, Belén Laspra, Glenn Branch, Carmelo Polino, Jordan S. Huffaker. Public acceptance of evolution in the United States, 1985–2020. Public Understanding of Science, 2021
21. Americans are creationists; Britons and Canadians side with evolution. Angus Reid Global. Vancouver, B.C.: Vision Critical. July 15, 2010
22. https://www.journalofcreation.com
23. Atkinson, G.D., *Impact of Weather on Military Operations: Past, Present, Future,* Defense Techical Information Center (US), 1973
24. Thinking, Fast and Slow, Daniel Kahneman, Penguin Books, May 2012
25. Alchemy: The Power of Ideas That Don't Make Sense, Rory Sutherland, WH Allen 2019
26. Estimating effects of individual-level workplace mental wellbeing interventions:Cross-sectional evidence from the UK, William Fleming, Wellbeing Research Centre, University of Oxford, April 2023
27. Deloitte.com: Poor mental health costs UK employers £51 billion a year for employees, 17th May 2024
28. Self-Determination Theory in Work Organizations: The State of a Science, Edward L. Deci1,2,3, Anja H. Olafsen2, and Richard M. Ryan, Annual Review of Organizational Psychology and Organizational Behavior, Volume 4, March 2017

2. CONTROL & COERCION: ORIGINS OF THE MODERN ORGANISATION

1. Sapiens: A Brief History of Humankind, Yuval Noah Harari, Vintage, April 2015
2. https://www.imdb.com/title/tt0167404/fullcredits
3. Credit and Blame at Work, Ben Dattner with Darren Dahl, Simon & Schuster, 2011
4. https://www.imdb.com/title/tt0386676/?ref_=ttawd_ov
5. https://en.wikipedia.org/wiki/Dilbert

3. POPULAR DECEPTIONS: PSEUDOSCIENCE & SUCCESS BOOKS

1. https://en.wikipedia.org/wiki/Scientific_method
2. https://blogs.ams.org/blogonmathblogs/2017/04/10/divorce-and-margarine/
3. Good To Great: Why Some Companies Make the Leap... and Others Don't, Jim Collins, Random House Business, October 2001
4. Luck Inc,. Drake Bennett, Boston Globe, April 13th 2009

5. From Good to Great to...Bruce G. Resnick and Timothy L. Smunt, Academy of Management Perspectives VOL. 22, NO. 4, November 2008

6. https://en.wikipedia.org/wiki/Gore-Tex

7. https://en.wikipedia.org/wiki/Post-it_note

8. https://en.wikipedia.org/wiki/Sildenafil

9. The Halo Effect: .and the Eight Other Business Delusions That Deceive Managers, Phil Rosenzweig, Simon & Schuster, May 2007

10. The Billion Dollar Secret: 20 Principles of Billionaire Wealth and Success, Rafael Badziag et al., Panoma Press, June 2019

11. The Diary of a CEO: The 33 Laws of Business and Life, Stephen Bartlett, Ebury Edge, August 2023

12. https://www.accenture.com/content/dam/accenture/final/capabilities/strategy-and-consulting/talent-and-organization/document/Accenture-CHRO-Growth-Executive.pdf

13. https://www.bcg.com/publications/2018/how-diverse-leadership-teams-boost-innovation

14. Gallup: The Relationship Between Engagement at Work and Organizational Outcomes Q12® Meta-Analysis: 11th Edition

15. https://www2.deloitte.com/us/en/insights/topics/leadership/digital-transformation-topics-for-corporate-technology-leadership.html

4. DRUNK ON THE LEADERSHIP KOOL-AID: A MODERN FAIRYTALE

1. The History of Cults: From Satanic Sects to the Manson Family, Robert Schroëder, Welbeck Publishing, June 2019

2. https://despair.com/collections/posters/products/meetings?variant=2457301507

3. https://www.gallup.com/workplace/506819/half-employees-looking-leave.aspx

4. Allison, Scott & Cecilione, Jennifer. (2015). Paradoxical Truths in Heroic Leadership: Implications for Leadership Development and Effectiveness

5. Leadership Matters: When, How Much, and How? Martin Reeves, Peter Tollman, Gerry Hansell, Kevin Whitaker, and Tom Deegan, BCG Henderson Institute, June 2020

6. https://www.businessinsider.com/reasons-executives-fail-2015-3

7. https://www.bcg.com/publications/2023/impact-of-ceo-first-100-days

8. https://www.equilar.com/reports/111-equilar-new-york-times-top-100-highest-paid-ceos-2024.html

9. Source: US Bureau of Labor Statistics

10. Reading leadership through Hegel's master/slave dialectic: Towards a theory of the powerlessness of the powerful, Harding N., Leadership, Volume10, Issue4, Page391-411, November 2014

11. https://www.mckinsey.com/capabilities/people-and-organizational-performance/our-insights/successful-transformations

12. Barends, E. and Rousseau, D. (2022) Organisational culture and performance: an evidence review. Scientific summary. London: Chartered Institute of Personnel and Development

13. King, David & Dalton, Dan & Daily, Catherine & Covin, Jeffrey. (2004). Meta-analyses of post-acquisition performance: Indications of unidentified moderators. Management Faculty Research and Publications. 25. 10.1002/smj.371

5. PRETENDING IT'S ALL RATIONAL: THE MBA GOGGLES

1. https://www.hbs.edu/about/history

2. Harvard Business School Website: https://www.hbs.edu/case-method-project/about/Pages/case-method-teaching.aspx

3. Collinson, David & Tourish, Dennis. (2015). Teaching Leadership Critically: New Directions for Leadership Pedagogy, Final Published Version. Academy of Management Learning and Education, The. 14. 576-594

4. Podolny, Joel. (2009). The buck stops (and starts) at business school. 87

5. Kweder, M. A. 2014. Whose welfare? A critical discourse analysis of Harvard Business Publishing cases. Paper presented at the annual meeting of the Academy of Management, Philadelphia

6. Starkey, K., & Tiratsoo, N. 2007. The business school and the bottom line. Cambridge, U.K.: Cambridge University Press

7. Grey, C. 2004. Reinventing business schools: The contribution of critical management education. Academy of Management Learning & Education, 3: 178–186

8. https://assets.publishing.service.gov.uk/media/5a7c46b940f0b6321db381b0/0532.pdf

9. Pascale, R. T. (1984). Perspectives on Strategy: The Real Story behind Honda's Success. California Management Review, 26(3), 47-72

10. Podolny, Joel. (2009). The buck stops (and starts) at business school. Harvard Business Review, June 2009

11. 2024 Report: Corporate Recruiters Survey, Graduate Management Admission Council, USA

6. THE FAD FACTORY: MANAGEMENT CONSULTANTS' REAL WORK

1. https://en.wikipedia.org/wiki/Bruce_Henderson

2. https://www.mckinsey.com/capabilities/strategy-and-corporate-finance/our-insights/enduring-ideas-the-7-s-framework

3. In Search Of Excellence: Lessons from America's Best-Run Companies, Robert H Waterman Jr, Tom Peters, Grand Central Publishing, August 1988

4. https://www.ft.com/content/d88492df-238d-4ff1-b8a4-1b4c9b117c6c

5. https://www2.deloitte.com/content/dam/Deloitte/us/Documents/technol ogy/us-ai-institute-what-is-the-metaverse-new.pdf
6. https://www.mckinsey.com/capabilities/growth-marketing-and-sales/our-insights/value-creation-in-the-metaverse
7. https://www.bbc.co.uk/news/technology-63488059
8. https://decentraland.org
9. https://www.sandbox.game/en/
10. https://investor.fb.com/investor-news/press-release-details/2021/Facebook-Reports-Third-Quarter-2021-Results/default.aspx
11. https://trends.google.co.uk/trends/explore?date=today%205-y&geo=GB&q= the%20metaverse&hl=en-GB
12. https://www.coingecko.com/research/publications/metaverse-land-prices
13. https://en.wikipedia.org/wiki/Dead_Parrot_sketch

7. NOT THE MESSIAH: SIMON SINEK & THE SOUNDBITE SELLERS

1. https://www.youtube.com/watch?v=u4ZoJKF_VuA&t=156s
2. Start With Why: How Great Leaders Inspire Everyone to Take Action, Simon Sinek, Penguin Books, October 2011
3. https://en.wikipedia.org/wiki/Hero's_journey
4. https://eu.usatoday.com/story/tech/2022/12/07/san-francisco-building-investi gate-twitter-bedrooms/10853609002/
5. https://www.newsweek.com/rankings/most-trustworthy-companies-amer ica-2024
6. https://www.qualtrics.com/blog/brands-with-most-loyal-customers/
7. https://www.schatz.senate.gov/imo/media/doc/Letter%20to%20Amazon% 20re%20worker%20surveillance%20FINAL.pdf

8. SELF-PROMOTING ECHO CHAMBERS: THE LINKEDIN EFFECT

1. Living in an Unreal World, Adam Curtis, 2016. See https://www.bbc.co.uk/programmes/p07d5yh3
2. https://blogs.lse.ac.uk/impactofsocialsciences/2024/05/01/why-is-vulnerabil ity-trending-on-linkedin/
3. https://www.independent.co.uk/life-style/ceo-linkedin-layoffs-crying-selfie-b2142626.html
4. https://www.helenjambunathan.com/

9. MODERN-DAY WITCHCRAFT:
CORPORATE CULTURE

1. https://www.english-heritage.org.uk/learn/histories/journey-into-witch craft-beliefs/
2. https://en.wikipedia.org/wiki/Elliott_Jaques
3. Defining Corporate Culture: How Social Scientists Define Culture, Values and Tradeoffs among Them, Daugherty, L. Working Paper 2007. LRN-RAND Center for Corporate Ethics, Law, and Governance
4. Graham, J.R., Harvey, C.R., Popadak, J. and Rajgopal, S. (2016) Corporate culture: evidence from the field. 27th Annual Conference on Financial Economics and Accounting Paper, Columbia Business School Research Paper No 16-49
5. https://committees.parliament.uk/committee/164/work-and-pensions-com mittee/news/97606/work-and-pensions-and-beis-committees-publish-report-on-carillion/
6. Barends, E. and Rousseau, D. (2022) Organisational culture and performance: an evidence review. Scientific summary. London: Chartered Institute of Personnel and Development

10. ASKING FOR TROUBLE:
POWER & HIERARCHY

1. Allison, Scott. (2023). Heroic Leadership. 10.1007/978-3-030-66252-3_2344.
2. Marlowe, F. (2005), Hunter-gatherers and human evolution, Evolutionary Anthropology, Vol. 14, Issue 2, pp. 54-67
3. Marlowe, F. (2004). The Hadza. In: Ember, C.R., Ember, M. (eds) Encyclopedia of Medical Anthropology. Springer, Boston, MA
4. The Dawn of Everything: A New History of Humanity, David Graeber & David Wengrow, Penguin Books, June 2022
5. https://en.wikipedia.org/wiki/Kondiaronk
6. From Benjamin Franklin to Peter Collinson, 9 May 1753, Founders Online, National Archives, https://founders.archives.gov/documents/Franklin/01-04-02-0173
7. Ashley J. Thomas, Vivian Mitchell, Emily Sumner, Brandon F. Terrizzi, Paul K. Piff, Barbara W. Sarnecka; Intuitive Sociology: *Children Recognize Decision-Making Structures and Prefer Groups With Less-Concentrated Power.* Open Mind 2022; 6 25–40
8. Higher social class predicts increased unethical behavior, Paul K. Piff, Daniel M. Stancato, Stéphane Côté, and Dacher Keltner, Proceedings of the National Academy of Sciences Vol. 109 | No. 11 March 13, 2012
9. Magee, J. C., & Smith, P. K. (2013). The social distance theory of power. Personality and Social Psychology Review, 17, 158–186

10. Goodwin, S. A., Gubin, A., Fiske, S. T., & Yzerbyt, V. Y. (2000). Power can bias impression processes: Stereotyping subordinates by default and by design. Group Processes & Intergroup R e l a t i o n s , 3 , 2 2 7 – 2 5 6

11. Guinote, A., Willis, G. B., & Martellotta, C. (2010). Social power increases implicit prejudice. Journal of Experimental Social Psychology, 46(2), 299–307

12. Koo, H. J., Piff, P. K., & Shariff, A. F. (2023). If I Could Do It, So Can They: Among the Rich, Those With Humbler Origins are Less Sensitive to the Difficulties of the Poor. Social Psychological and Personality Science, 14(3), 333-341

13. Erik Gonzalez-Mulé, Bethany S. Cockburn. This job is (literally) killing me: A moderated-mediated model linking work characteristics to mortality.. Journal of Applied Psychology, 2020

14. D. Keltner, D.H. Gruenfeld, C. Anderson. Power, approach, and inhibition. Psychological Review, 110 (2) (2003), pp. 265-284

15. Gray, J. A. (1987). "The neuropsychology of emotion and personality," in Cognitive Neurochemistry, eds S. M. Stahl, S. D. Iversen, and E. C. Goodman (New York: Oxford University Press), 171–190

16. Huisi (Jessica) Li, Ya-Ru Chen, John Angus D. Hildreth (2022) Powerlessness Also Corrupts: Lower Power Increases Self-Promotional Lying. Organization Science 34(4):1422-1440

17. Kras, Kimberly & Portillo, Shannon & Taxman, Faye. (2017). Managing from the Middle: Frontline Supervisors and Perceptions of Their Organizational Power. Law & Policy. 39. 10.1111/lapo.12079

18. Leading Systems: Lessons from the Power Lab, Barry Oshry, Berrett-Koehler Publishers; First Edition (September 1, 1999)

11. MEANINGLESS ABSTRACTIONS: VISION, PURPOSE & VALUES

1. https://en.wikipedia.org/wiki/History_of_Nokia

2. Water and sewerage companies in England: environmental performance report 2023, Environment Agency

3. http://www.damicofcg.com/files/74720/Vision%20%26%20Values.pdf

4. PwC's 27th Annual Global CEO Survey, https://www.pwc.com/us/en/executive-leadership-hub/ceo.html

5. Larsson, A. (2019), *The seven dimensions of Skunk Works: a new approach and what makes it unique*, Journal of Research in Marketing and Entrepreneurship, Vol. 21 No. 1, pp. 37-54

12. LAZY AND INFANTILISING:
THE ENGAGEMENT SURVEY

1. https://hbr.org/2019/05/where-measuring-engagement-goes-wrong
2. Iaffaldano, Michelle & Muchinsky, Paul. (1985). Job Satisfaction and Job Performance. A Meta-Analysis. Psychological Bulletin. 97. 251-273. 10.1037/0033-2909.97.2.251
3. Kahn, W. A. (1990). Psychological conditions of personal engagement and disengagement at work. Academy of Management Journal, 33(4), 692–724. https://doi.org/10.2307/256287
4. Source: CIPD/High Pay Centre (2020)
5. Gifford, J. and Young, J. (2021) Employee engagement: definitions, measures and outcomes. Discussion report. London: Chartered Institute of Personnel and Development
6. Guest, D. (2014) Employee engagement: fashionable fad or long-term fixture? In: Truss, C., Alfes, K., Delbridge, R., Shantz, A. and Soane, E. (eds) Employee engagement in theory and practice (pp235–49). Abingdon: Routledge
7. Evaluating the evidence on employee engagement and its potential benefits to NHS staff: a synthesis of the literature. Catherine Bailey, Adrian Madden, Kerstin Alfes, Luke Fletcher, Dilys Robinson, Jenny Holmes, Jonathan Buzzeo, Graeme Currie
8. Reid, C. A., & Short, S. D. (2024). Cautionary comments on the clifton-strengths assessment in higher education. *Consulting Psychology Journal,* 76(3), 313–330

13. CAREFUL WHAT YOU WISH
FOR: BREAKING DOWN SILOS

1. https://hbr.org/2024/05/why-employees-who-work-across-silos-get-burned-out

15. A COTTAGE INDUSTRY OF FAILURE:
THE GOVERNANCE ILLUSION

1. *Conducting Effective Board Assessments,* PWC Govenance Insights Centre, January 2023
2. https://rooseveltinstitute.org/wp-content/uploads/2020/07/RI-Fighting-Short-Termism-201710.pdf
3. https://www.theqca.com/
4. Source: Advisor Rankings data https://www.adviser-rankings.com/advisers/auditors
5. https://auditreformlab.group.shef.ac.uk/

17. WHERE DUMB IDEAS MEET
FAKE CONSENSUS: THE MEETING

1. The Surprising Science of Meetings: How You Can Lead Your Team to Peak Performance, Stephen G. Rogelberg, OUP USA, April 2019

2. Porter, Michael E., and Nitin Nohria. "How CEOs Manage Time." Harvard Business Review 96, no. 4 (July–August 2018): 42–51

3. See: Grandey A. A. (2003). When "the show must go on": Surface acting and deep acting as determinants of emotional exhaustion and peer-rated service delivery. Academy of Management Journal, 46, 86-96.

4. Shumski Thomas, J., Olien, J. L., Allen, J. A., Rogelberg, S. G., & Kello, J. E. (2018). Faking It for the Higher-Ups: Status and Surface Acting in Workplace Meetings. Group & Organization Management, 43(1), 72-100

5. Bryant M., Cox J. W. (2006). The expression of suppression: Loss and emotional labour in narratives of organisational change. Journal of Management & Organization, 12, 116-130.

6. Jones E. E., Pittman T. S. (1982). Toward a general theory of strategic self-presentation. In Suls J. (Ed.), Psychological perspectives on the self (Vol. 1, pp. 231-262). Hillsdale, NJ: Lawrence Erlbaum

7. Kauffeld, S. and Lehmann-Willenbrock, N. (2012) Meetings matter: Effects of team meetings on team and organizational success. Small Group Research. Vol 43, No 2, pp130–58

8. Klein, G. (2007). "Performing a Project Premortem". Harvard Business Review. 85 (9): 18–19

18. CONFUSION IN ACTION:
THE DIVERSITY AGENDA

1. https://www.kornferry.com/insights/this-week-in-leadership/your-chief-diversity-officer-is-likely-leaving

2. Report: Global Diversity and Inclusion (D&I) Market 2024, Global Industry Analysts Inc.

3. Green, Jeremiah and Hand, John R. M., Diversity Matters/Delivers/Wins Revisited in S&P 500® Firms (August 6, 2021). Available at https://ssrn.com/abstract=3849562

4. https://fortune.com/2022/05/18/problem-diversity-inclusion-initiatives-dei-women-careers-work-leadership-stereotypes-michele-frank/

5. Farrell, Anne M., and Michele L. Frank. "It's complicated: How a subordinate's gender influences supervisors' use of past performance information when appraising potential." Journal of Management Accounting Research 34.2 (2022): 137-161

6. https://nypost.com/2021/02/23/coca-cola-diversity-training-urged-workers-to-be-less-white/

7. https://www.bbc.co.uk/news/uk-66060490

8. Dobbin, F., &; Kalev, A. (2016). Why diversity programs fail. Harvard Business Review, 94(7/8), 52-60

9. Anand, R., & Winters, M. F. (2008). A retrospective view of corporate diversity training from 1964 to the present. Academy of Management Learning & Education, 7(3)

10. https://assets.publishing.service.gov.uk/government/uploads/system/uploads/attachment_data/file/944431/20-12-14_UBT_BIT_report.pdf

11. Iris Bohnet, Alexandra van Geen, and Max Bazerman, "When Performance Trumps Gender Bias: Joint Versus Separate Evaluation," Management Science 62, no. 5 (2016): 1225–1234

12. Edward H. Chang, Erika L. Kirgios, Aneesh Rai, Katherine L. Milkman (2020) The Isolated Choice Effect and Its Implications for Gender Diversity in Organizations. Management Science 66(6):2752-2761

19. POINTLESS AT BEST: THE PERFORMANCE APPRAISAL

1. Drive: The Surprising Truth About What Motivates Us, Daniel H. Pink, Riverhead Books, 2009

2. Kerr, S (1975). On the Folly of Rewarding A, While Hoping for B. Ohio State University

3. Individual or Team-Based Incentives? When to Use One, the Other... or Both, Incentive Research Foundation, September 2021

4. Kluger, A.N. and Denisi, A. (1996) The effects of feedback interventions on performance: a historical review, a meta-analysis, and a preliminary feedback intervention theory. Psychological Bulletin. Vol 119, No 2. p254

5. *Could do better? Assessing what works in performance management*, CIPD 2016

6. Georgesen, J.C. and Harris, M.J. (1998) Why's my boss always holding me down? A meta-analysis of power effects on performance evaluations. Personality and Social Psychology Review. Vol 2, No 3. pp184–95

7. Latham, G.P., Budworth, M.-H., Yanar, B. and Whyte, G. (2008) The influence of a manager's own performance appraisal on the evaluation of others. International Journal of Selection and Assessment. Vol 16, No 3. pp220–28

8. Slaughter, J.E. and Greguras, G.J. (2008) Bias in performance ratings: clarifying the role of positive versus negative escalation. Human Performance. Vol 21, No 4. pp414–26

9. Sutton, A.W., Baldwin, S.P., Wood, L. and Hoffman, B.J. (2013) A meta-analysis of the relationship between rater liking and performance ratings. Human Performance. Vol 26, No 5. pp409–29

10. Gordan, R.A. (1996) Impact of ingratiation on judgments and evaluations: a meta-analytic investigation. Journal of Personality and Social Psychology. Vol 71. pp54–70

11. Higgins, C.A., Judge, T.A. and Ferris, G.R. (2003) Influence tactics and work outcomes: a meta-analysis. Journal of Organizational Behavior. Vol 24. pp89–106

12. Huang, G.-H., Xiong-Ying, N., Zhao, H.H., Ashford, S.J. and Lee, C. (2013) Reducing job insecurity and increasing performance rating: Does impression management matter? Journal of Applied Psychology. Vol 98, No 5. pp852–62

13. Reinventing Organizations: A Guide to Creating Organizations Inspired by the Next Stage in Human Consciousness, Laloux, F., (2014) Nelson Parker

20. GREENWASHING AND HOT AIR: THE "E" IN ESG

1. https://www.ethicalconsumer.org/research-hub/uk-ethical-consumer-markets-report

2. Gerber, P. J., H.Steinfeld, B.Henderson, A.Mottet, C.Opio, J.Dijkman, A.Falcucci, and G.Tempio. 2013. Tackling climate change through livestock: a global assessment of emissions and mitigation opportunities. Rome: FAO

3. https://brandaudit.breakfreefromplastic.org/brand-audit-2023/

4. https://changingmarkets.org

5. Source: Greenpeace / The Last Beach Cleanup and Beyond Plastics, 2022, pp. 2–3

6. Oreskes N., Conway E. M. (2010). Merchants of doubt: How a handful of scientists obscured the truth on issues from tobacco smoke to global warming (1st U.S. ed.). Bloomsbury Press

7. Supran G., Rahmstorf S., Oreskes N. (2023). Assessing ExxonMobil's global warming projections. Science, 379(6628), Article eabk0063

8. https://www.bp.com/en/global/corporate/news-and-insights/press-releases/bp-update-on-strategic-progress.html

9. Flowers M. E., Matisoff D. C., Noonan D. S. (2020). In the LEED: Racing to the top in environmental self-regulation. Business Strategy and the Environment, 29(6), 2842–2856

10. Liute A., De Giacomo M. R. (2022). The environmental performance of UK-based B Corp companies: An analysis based on the triple bottom line approach. Business Strategy and the Environment, 31(3), 810–827

21. DANGEROUS ARTEFACTS: THE ORGANISATION CHART & OTHER VOODOO

1. Girod, Stéphane & Karim, Samina. (2017). Restructure or Reconfigure: Designing the reorg that works for you. Harvard Business Review. 95. 128-132

2. Chaddha, V., Corporate restructuring and its effect on employee morale and performance, International Journal of Research in IT, Management and Engineering, Volume 6 Issue 05, May 2016, Page6-14

22. STUPIDITY AT SCALE: THE
TRANSFORMATION PROGRAMME

1. https://www.sbs.ox.ac.uk/sites/default/files/2024-04/2024-ey-report.pdf
2. SAVING A COMPANY TRANSFORMATION FROM THE BRINK OF FAILURE. Getting to the root of why transformations go off track. Hector S. Nelson, Rutger von Post, and Julia Cormier. Oliver Wyman.
3. https://en.wikipedia.org/wiki/Dave_Snowden
4. Snowden, David (1999). "Liberating Knowledge", in Liberating Knowledge. CBI Business Guide. London: Caspian Publishing

23. A QUICK PRIMER:
WHAT IS GENERATIVE AI?

1. https://www.nytimes.com/2023/06/08/nyregion/lawyer-chatgpt-sanctions.html
2. https://www.mckinsey.com/mgi/our-research/a-new-future-of-work-the-race-to-deploy-ai-and-raise-skills-in-europe-and-beyond

24. THE TURING TRAP: WHY CEOS
NEED TO TREAD CAREFULLY

1. https://www.safe.ai/work/statement-on-ai-risk
2. Brynjolfsson, Erik. (2022). The Turing Trap: The Promise & Peril of Human-Like Artificial Intelligence. Daedalus. 151. 272-287

26. THE CON OF EARLY
ADOPTION: CAUTIONARY TALES

1. https://zillow.mediaroom.com/2021-02-25-Zillow-Starts-Making-Cash-Offers-For-the-Zestimate
2. https://edition.cnn.com/2021/11/02/homes/zillow-exit-ibuying-home-business/index.html
3. https://themarkup.org/
4. https://themarkup.org/news/2024/03/29/nycs-ai-chatbot-tells-businesses-to-break-the-law
5. https://www.nyc.gov/assets/oti/downloads/pdf/reports/artificial-intelligence-action-plan.pdf
6. https://www.tiktok.com/@typical_redhead_/video/7192248491853303086?amp%3Bt=1676307505881&q=robot%20mcdonalds%20fail
7. https://decisions.civilresolutionbc.ca/crt/crtd/en/item/525448/index.do
8. https://futurism.com/sports-illustrated-ai-generated-writers

9. https://web.archive.org/web/20221205082417/https://www.si.com/review/author/drewortiz/

28. THE PRESSING NEED TO REINVENT HR

1. https://www.linkedin.com/business/talent/blog/talent-analytics/types-of-jobs-with-most-turnover
2. https://hateithere.co/podcast/
3. The Organized Mind: The Science of Preventing Overload, Increasing Productivity and Restoring Your Focus, Daniel Leviton, Penguin, June 2015
4. Barends E, Villanueva J, Rousseau DM, Briner RB, Jepsen DM, Houghton E, et al. (2017) Managerial attitudes and perceived barriers regarding evidence-based practice: An international survey. PLoS ONE 12(10): e0184594

29. THE IMPORTANCE OF CRITICAL THINKING

1. Armstrong, P. (2010). Bloom's Taxonomy. Vanderbilt University Center for Teaching

30. THE CASE FOR GREATER AUTONOMY

1. https://www3.weforum.org/docs/WEF_Future_of_Jobs_2023.pdf
2. The Decision Maker: Unlock the Potential of Everyone in Your Organization, One Decision at a Time, Dennis Bakke, Pear Press,March 2003
3. https://jobs.netflix.com/culture
4. Power Can Corrupt Leaders. Compassion Can Save Them, Rasmus Hougaard, Jacqueline Carter, and Louise Chester, Harvard Business Review, February 15th 2018
5. Source: Buurtzorg.com August 2024
6. https://jobs.netflix.com/culture
7. See www.disrupt.co for resources
8. See https://www.holacracy.org/ for details

32. LESSONS FROM DESIGN THINKING

1. https://hbr.org/2008/06/design-thinking
2. Solving Problems with Design Thinking, 10 Stories of What Works, Liedtka, J., King A., and Bennett, K. Columbia Business School Publishing, 2013

ABOUT THE AUTHOR

Paul D. Sweeney is an author and strategist. Formerly an independent strategic advisor to multiple FTSE businesses, Paul was Chief Strategy Officer at Unite Group PLC (FTSE100) from 2020-2023 and is a fellow of the RSA (Royal Society for the Encouragement of Arts, Manufactures and Commerce).

He is currently the CEO at Sense Labs, a London-based advisory firm that helps CEOs improve performance by freeing their people from pointless nonsense, simplifying structures, and uncovering hidden talent.

Known for his fondness for disruptive thinking, Paul's random career path took him from university dropout to his first job in an airline's lost luggage department. After multiple operations and general management roles in aviation, Paul completed an Executive MBA at London Business School. This was followed by a three-year stint in a start-up and, later, a serendipitous career as a consultant, strategic advisor and FTSE100 executive.

Paul lives with his family in Richmond, Southwest London, and is an avid sailor and sea kayaker.

He can be contacted by email at: paul@senselabs.co